CIVIL WAR
—NORTHERN—
VIRGINIA 1861

WILLIAM S. CONNERY

THE
History
PRESS

Published by The History Press
Charleston, SC 29403
www.historypress.net

Copyright © 2011 by William S. Connery
All rights reserved

Images are from the author's collection unless otherwise noted.

Front cover: *First Battle Flags*, by Don Troiani.
Back cover: Tinted lithograph, *The Death of Ellsworth*.
Facing page: Modern map of Northern Virginia.

First published 2011
Second printing 2013
Third printing 2013
Fourth printing 2013

Manufactured in the United States

978.1.60949.352.3

Library of Congress Cataloging-in-Publication Data

Connery, William S.
Civil War Northern Virginia 1861 / William S. Connery.
p. cm.
Includes bibliographical references and index.
ISBN 978-1-60949-352-3
1. Virginia--History--Civil War, 1861-1865--Campaigns. 2. Virginia, Northern--History,
Military--19th century. 3. United States--History--Civil War, 1861-1865--Campaigns. I.
Title.
E470.2.C716 2011
975.5'03--dc23
2011044585

Notice: The information in this book is true and complete to the best of our knowledge. It is
offered without guarantee on the part of the author or The History Press. The author and
The History Press disclaim all liability in connection with the use of this book.

All rights reserved. No part of this book may be reproduced or transmitted in any form
whatsoever without prior written permission from the publisher except in the case of brief
quotations embodied in critical articles and reviews.

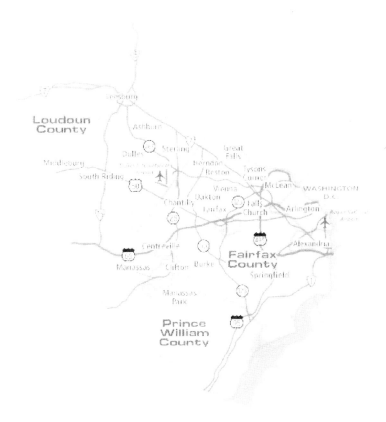

Oh thus be it ever,
When freemen shall stand,
Between their loved homes and the war's desolation.
Blest with vict'ry and peace,
May the Heav'n rescued land,
Praise the Power that hath made and preserved us a nation!
Then conquer we must,
When our cause it is just,
And this be our motto, "In God Is Our Trust"

—Written by a Georgetown lawyer in Baltimore Harbor, 1814

Contents

Preface

L etter written for the 1911 *Photographic History of the Civil War*:

The White House
Washington

We have reached a point in this country when we can look back, not without love, not without intense pride, but without partisan passion, to the events of the Civil War. We have reached a point, I am glad to say, when the North can admire to the full the heroes of the South, and the South admire to the full the heroes of the North. There is a monument in Quebec that always commended itself to me—a monument to commemorate the battle of the Plains of Abraham. On one face of that beautiful structure is the name of Montcalm, and on the opposite side the name of Wolfe. That always seemed to me to be the acme of what we ought to reach in this country; and I am glad to say that in my own alma mater, Yale, we have established an association for the purpose of erecting within her academic precincts a memorial not to the Northern Yale men who died, nor to the Southern Yale men who died; but to the Yale men who died in the Civil War...William Howard Taft

The Yale Civil War Memorial was dedicated on June 20, 1915, and is located in the Memorial (Woolsey) Hall Rotunda at Yale University, at the intersection of Grove and College Streets in New Haven, Connecticut.

President William Howard Taft. He supported the Peace Festival in Manassas, Virginia, in 1911 to bring final healing to the nation. *Courtesy of the Library of Congress.*

The fact that the Yale Memorial commemorates the dead of both Union and Confederate forces is out of the ordinary and unique in Connecticut. President Taft's father, Alphonso Taft, was secretary of war and attorney general under President U.S. Grant.

Introduction

It is difficult to believe. Every weekday, drivers come into Washington, D.C., from all directions. Most from the south funnel into I-395, which takes the occupants to their jobs at the Pentagon and downtown D.C. to the alphabet soup of government agencies: DOA, DOE, FBI, DOI, DOS, etc. As the highway nears the Pentagon, it actually goes over the site of one of the forts established in 1861 to protect the Southern Gate to Washington. In some ways, the city has not changed much since the days of John Fitzgerald Kennedy, who called it "a city of Northern charm and Southern efficiency."

My father was a World War II vet, having fought in New Guinea and the Philippines as part of the Sixth U.S. Army, Artillery. I came along late in the 1940s, part of the Baby Boom. I grew up close to Washington, in Baltimore, and my family would often take the drive over to D.C. Those were the days before the Air and Space Museum, when the Wright Brothers' Flyer was hanging from the ceiling of the Smithsonian Castle. My first visit to the White House was in 1962, when our man (JFK) was president. Back in the day when being IrishCatholicDemocrat was all one word. I remember "duck and cover"; I was going to elementary school near Friendship (now BWI–Thurgood Marshall) Airport during the Cuban Missile Crisis of October 1962. We thought the world was ending then. I was just starting high school when JFK was assassinated—we prayed for the repose of his soul, and I remember the silent bus trip from Baltimore to Glen Burnie to tell my family the news.

This same period (1961–65) was the time of the centennial of the Civil War. I traveled with my family up to Gettysburg, Antietam and Harpers Ferry. I still have a "genuine, authentic Civil War bullet" from the National Tower in Gettysburg. Even today, driving into Harpers Ferry is like going 150 years into the past. The last veterans of that conflict passed away in the 1950s. This was within my lifetime! I remember my high school history teacher, who was from Pennsylvania, in the mid-1960s telling the class that Robert E. Lee was a traitor. Most of us rebelled against that.

I've been often asked about my interest in the Civil War. I speak to many groups in the D.C. area, and most have an ancestor—sometimes two or two dozen—who was a proud Reb or Yank, or both. How about Bill Connery? Well, my mother's parents got off the boat in Baltimore from Krakow (the same part of Poland as Blessed John Paul II) in the 1890s and settled in Fells Point, where Maryland's feisty Senator Barbara Mikulski hails from. My great-grandfather John Connery (yes, the same name as the Scottish actor Sir Sean—his ancestry is Irish, although he was born in Scotland, and he received his only Oscar for playing an Irish cop in *The Untouchables*) came from Waterford in Ireland and settled in Baltimore in the mid-1860s, first joining the U.S. Army, after the war, and then the Baltimore City Police Department. As far as I know, I have no dog in the fight of the War Between the States.

What I do have is the timing of my birth—January 19—which I share with Confederate general in chief Robert E. Lee. It is also the birthday of Edgar Allan Poe, who happens to be buried in Baltimore. Being from Charm City, I try to keep neutral in our great internecine fight, although I am a Unionist at heart. Just don't call me a Yankee!

My desire in this book is to relate some of the known and lesser-known events that transpired in Northern Virginia in 1861 and the chaos and uncertainty of that time. The area is now one of the richest and highly populated areas in the United States. At the start of the "Recent Unpleasantness" in 1861, the area contained small villages like Fairfax Court House, Falls Church, Vienna, McLean, Brentsville and Leesburg. Alexandria was a metropolis of twelve thousand souls. Most of the area was farmland, which had been advertised in the Northern papers and journals. Thus, Pennsylvania Dutch, Quakers and hardy New Englanders had recently come to the area, attracted to the cheap land and proximity to the port of Alexandria and the nation's capital, known at that time as Washington City. About the only thing in Arlington was the mansion and eleven-hundred-acre estate of Colonel and Mrs. Robert

Map of Northern Virginia in 1861. Farmland predominated where highways and townhouses now exist.

E. Lee. Arlington and Alexandria City were combined in Alexandria County, until the city split off in 1870 and the county changed its name to Arlington County in 1920.

Two counties that have kept most of their antique charms are Loudoun and Prince William Counties. The counties of Fairfax and Loudoun now usually rank in the top five of richest counties in America. Things were much different in 1861 and the years that followed. The first major battle of the war was fought in Northern Virginia in July 1861, close to the railroad station of Manassas Junction and a little creek called Bull Run, and is being covered in another book.

A TASTE OF THINGS TO COME

July 1860: The Occoquan Flag Incident

An introduction to the heated emotions of the era can be found in the village of Occoquan, just within Prince William County on the border with Fairfax County. On July 4, 1860, as the November presidential elections were drawing closer, a group of Republicans got together on the Rockledge property and raised a political banner embossed with the names of Abraham (Abram) Lincoln and Hannibal Hamlin. The group paraded with their muskets and threatened anyone who voiced disapproval of their Liberty Pole.

George Potter of Fairfax, captain of the Sixteenth Virginia Militia, wrote to the adjutant general in Richmond on July 18 asking if the pole and flag, having been raised in a Southern state, should be pulled down. Captain Potter and his neighbors saw this as a bold step toward abolition. The letter was forwarded to Governor John Letcher, who on the twenty-third sent a dispatch to Colonel William G. Brawner of the Thirty-sixth Regiment of Prince William County. The governor wrote that if the people tolerated the banner, the governor had no authority in the matter. But if the arms being used belonged to the state, they should be confiscated and returned to Richmond.

When the Prince William County officials next met in Brentsville at the county courthouse, it was decided that the flag and pole were an insult to the people of Virginia; therefore, the offensive banner should be removed. The decision was made to send troops to Occoquan on July 27 to guarantee that the Liberty Pole and Lincoln Banner were destroyed. One of the Republicans, William Athey, when he heard of the intended flagpole destruction, wired Governor Letcher for protection of the property and people of Occoquan. He pleaded that the good people of the village were about to be descended upon by a mob of three hundred men from a distant part of the county at noon on Friday the twenty-seventh because of their political opinions.

The governor's office fired off a message to General Eppa Hunton of Prince William County. General Hunton was told that as attorney for the commonwealth it was up to him to maintain civil obedience, and if he determined this was not possible, then a military force should be called out in sufficient number to maintain it. Athey's request was not well received in Richmond, and the governor's office said the entreaty by Athey to protect the traitors who had raised the Lincoln Banner was "about the

Commonwealth of Virginia attorney Eppa Hunton. In 1860, he was also a general in a local Prince William County militia company.

most consummate piece of impudence and audacity that has ever come under our notice."

The Prince William Militia, led by Captain William W. Thornton, arrived at 3:30 p.m. on the twenty-seventh, arranged themselves silently around the Liberty Pole and remained so during the events. The U.S. flag was flying along with the Lincoln Banner, but the hopes of protecting their freedom

The campaign banner of candidate Abram Lincoln, which caused such a fuss in Prince William County in July 1860.

with the Stars and Stripes were dashed. A company of forty soldiers led by Captain Fitzhugh soon followed the militia. The soldiers formed in a square around the pole, seemingly ignoring the militia from Brentsville.

Joseph Janney, a local miller and merchant, stepped forward and asked that his property be protected. Janney argued that he did not hold the same opinions as the Republicans but insisted that he had approved the use of his property. A number of people had signed a petition requesting the protection of the flagpole and presented it to Captain Thornton. The request was ignored, and when the command was given, James W. Jackson of Fairfax came forward from the troop formation and gave the first axe blow to the pole. The Republicans stood around and jeered the soldiers, and when the destruction of the banner and pole was complete, the troop departed, taking the U.S. flag, Lincoln campaign banner and pole pieces with them to Brentsville. Others in the crowd displaying Southern sentiment applauded the soldiers at the removal of the flagpole and standards.

That evening, there was a personal confrontation between Colonel Brawner, who resided south of Occoquan, and Mr. Janney. It was said that Janney did not have any better outcome in this showdown that ended in blows than he'd had in the one earlier in the day. The crowd went home as night approached, but the village of Occoquan had gained a reputation as a home for Republicans and abolitionists. In the November 1860 presidential election, only 55 votes were for Lincoln, out of 1,042 total votes in Prince William County. All of those Lincoln votes were cast in Occoquan. In comparison, Lincoln had received 2 votes in Alexandria County, 24 votes in Fairfax County and 11 votes in Loudoun County. Other Virginia localities, such as Clarke, Culpeper, Frederick, Madison, Orange and Stafford Counties, had cast 0 votes for Lincoln. Also, Mr. Jackson will make an important appearance later in our narrative.

1

The Deep South Leaves

Virginia Holds Steady

It is important to remember that the 1860 presidential election was divided among four candidates. The Democratic Party had split between Southern candidate John Breckinridge of Kentucky and Northern candidate Stephen Douglas of Illinois. Another party, the Constitutional Union, put forth John Bell of Tennessee. Abraham Lincoln of Illinois ran as a Republican in just that party's second national election (John C. Fremont had lost to Democrat James Buchanan in 1856). No Democrat supported President Buchanan for a second term. Buchanan was considered a "doughface"—a Northerner with Southern sympathies. As 1861 dawned, Northern Virginia was keeping its powder dry, especially concerning events in the Deep South. The last Virginian to become president (not by election but because of the untimely death of Old Tippecanoe, William Henry Harrison, in 1841), John Tyler contemplated a bleak future from his plantation, Sherwood Forest, along the James River between Richmond and Williamsburg. Lincoln's election cast Tyler into gloom. He had written to a friend after the November election, "All is over, and Lincoln elected. South Carolina will secede. Virginia will abide developments. For myself, I rest in quiet, and shall do so unless I see my poor opinions have due weight."

Lincoln's name was not even on the South Carolina ballot or that of other states in the Deep South. Even in Virginia, out of 166,891 votes cast, Lincoln had received just 1,887, and most of those were from the western part of the state. On receiving the news of Lincoln's election, the South Carolina legislature called a special state convention to meet in Charleston. On December 20, by unanimous vote, South Carolina seceded from the Union:

> *The people of the State of South Carolina, in Convention assembled, on the 26th day of April, A.D., 1852, declared that the frequent violations of the Constitution of the United States, by the Federal Government, and its encroachments upon the reserved rights of the States, fully justified this State in then withdrawing from the Federal Union; but in deference to the opinions and wishes of the other slaveholding States, she forbore at that time to exercise this right. Since that time, these encroachments have continued to increase, and further forbearance ceases to be a virtue...*
>
> *We, therefore, the People of South Carolina, by our delegates in Convention assembled, appealing to the Supreme Judge of the world for the rectitude of our intentions, have solemnly declared that the Union heretofore existing between this State and the other States of North America, is dissolved, and that the State of South Carolina has resumed her position among the nations of the world, as a separate and independent State; with full power to levy war, conclude peace, contract alliances, establish commerce, and to do all other acts and things which independent States may of right do.*

James L. Petigru, a South Carolinian lawyer, politician and jurist, best known for his service as the state's attorney general, uttered his famous (or infamous) words after his state's secession: "South Carolina is too small for a republic and too large for an insane asylum." This quote is still used to describe politics in the Palmetto State. South Carolina was briefly a republic until it joined the Confederacy in February 1861.

Conventions of delegates were meeting in the other Southern states. On January 9, Mississippi seceded. Its Declaration focuses on the overriding importance of slavery:

> *In the momentous step which our State has taken of dissolving its connection with the government of which we so long formed a part, it is but just that we should declare the prominent reasons which have induced our course.*
>
> *Our position is thoroughly identified with the institution of slavery—the greatest material interest of the world. Its labor supplies the product which constitutes by far the largest and most important portions of commerce of the earth. These products are peculiar to the climate verging on the tropical regions, and by an imperious law of nature, none but the black race can*

THE

UNION

IS

DISSOLVED!

Passed unanimously at 1.15 o'clock, P. M., December 20th, 1860.

AN ORDINANCE

To dissolve the Union between the State of South Carolina and other States united with her under the compact entitled "The Constitution of the United States of America."

CHARLESTON

MERCURY

EXTRA

Broadside of the *Charleston Mercury* proclaiming South Carolina's leaving the Union.

bear exposure to the tropical sun. These products have become necessities of the world, and a blow at slavery is a blow at commerce and civilization. That blow has been long aimed at the institution, and was at the point of reaching its consummation. There was no choice left us but submission to the mandates of abolition, or dissolution of the Union, whose principles had been subverted to work out our ruin.

Florida followed on January 10:

> *We, the people of the State of Florida, in convention assembled, do solemnly ordain, publish, and declare, That the State of Florida hereby withdraws herself from the confederacy of States existing under the name of the United States of America and from the existing Government of the said States; and that all political connection between her and the Government of said States ought to be, and the same is hereby, totally annulled, and said Union of States dissolved; and the State of Florida is hereby declared a sovereign and independent nation; and that all ordinances heretofore adopted, in so far as they create or recognize said Union, are rescinded; and all laws or parts of laws in force in this State, in so far as they recognize or assent to said Union, be, and they are hereby, repealed.*

Alabama seceded on January 11 and called for a convention of the slave states:

> *AN ORDINANCE to dissolve the union between the State of Alabama and the other States united under the compact styled "The Constitution of the United States of America."*
>
> *Whereas, the election of Abraham Lincoln and Hannibal Hamlin to the offices of president and vice-president of the United States of America, by a sectional party, avowedly hostile to the domestic institutions and to the peace and security of the people of the State of Alabama, preceded by many and dangerous infractions of the constitution of the United States by many of the States and people of the Northern section, is a political wrong of so insulting and menacing a character as to justify the people of the State of Alabama in the adoption of prompt and decided measures for their future peace and security, therefore:*
>
> *Be it declared and ordained by the people of the State of Alabama, in Convention assembled, That the State of Alabama now withdraws, and is hereby withdrawn from the Union known as "the United States of America," and henceforth ceases to be one of said United States, and is, and of right ought to be a Sovereign and Independent State...*
>
> *Be it resolved by the people of Alabama in Convention assembled, That the people of the States of Delaware, Maryland, Virginia, North Carolina, South Carolina, Florida, Georgia, Mississippi, Louisiana, Texas, Arkansas, Tennessee, Kentucky and Missouri, be and are hereby invited to meet the people of the State of Alabama, by their Delegates, in Convention,*

on the 4ᵗʰ day of February, A.D., 1861, at the city of Montgomery, in the State of Alabama, for the purpose of consulting with each other as to the most effectual mode of securing concerted and harmonious action in whatever measures may be deemed most desirable for our common peace and security.

Georgia seceded on January 19, which happened to be Lieutenant Colonel Robert E. Lee's fifty-fourth birthday:

We the people of the State of Georgia in Convention assembled do declare and ordain that the ordinance adopted by the State of Georgia in convention on the 2ⁿᵈ day of Jany. in the year of our Lord seventeen hundred and eighty-eight, whereby the constitution of the United States of America was assented to, ratified and adopted, and also all acts and parts of acts of the general assembly of this State, ratifying and adopting amendments to said constitution, are hereby repealed, rescinded and abrogated.

We do further declare and ordain that the union now existing between the State of Georgia and other States under the name of the United States of America is hereby dissolved, and that the State of Georgia is in full possession and exercise of all those rights of sovereignty which belong and appertain to a free and independent State.

Louisiana followed suit on January 26:

Aɴ ᴏʀᴅɪɴᴀɴᴄᴇ to dissolve the union between the State of Louisiana and other States united with her under the compact entitled "The Constitution of the United States of America."

We, the people of the State of Louisiana, in convention assembled, do declare and ordain, and it is hereby declared and ordained, That the ordinance passed by us in convention on the 22d day of November, in the year eighteen hundred and eleven, whereby the Constitution of the United States of America and the amendments of the said Constitution were adopted, and all laws and ordinances by which the State of Louisiana became a member of the Federal Union, be, and the same are hereby, repealed and abrogated; and that the union now subsisting between Louisiana and other States under the name of "The United States of America" is hereby dissolved.

Meanwhile, on January 29, Kansas entered the Union as the thirty-fourth state. The Wyandotte (Kansas) Constitution was approved in a referendum

Governor Sam Houston of Texas. He refused to take the oath of loyalty to the Confederacy and predicted doom for the young nation. *Courtesy of the Library of Congress.*

by a vote of 10,421 to 5,530 on October 4, 1859. During the mid- to late 1850s, "Bleeding Kansas" had been a battleground between pro- and antislavery forces. In April 1860, the U.S. House of Representatives voted 134 to 73 to admit Kansas under the Wyandotte Constitution; however, there was resistance in the U.S. Senate. As slave states seceded from the Union, their senators left their seats, and on January 21, 1861, the Senate passed the Kansas bill. Slavery was directly prohibited under Section 6: "There shall be no slavery in this State, and no involuntary servitude, except for the punishment of crime, whereof the party shall have been duly convicted."

On February 1, Texas became the last (seventh) state of the Deep South to leave the Union. While the governors of the other seceding states supported their leaving the Union, such was not the case with Texan governor Sam Houston. Although Houston was a slave owner and opposed abolition, he opposed the secession of Texas from the Union. At this point, Houston was almost seventy and had been the first president of the Republic of Texas in the 1830s.

Houston refused to recognize its legality, but the Texas legislature upheld the legitimacy of secession. The political forces that brought about Texas's secession were powerful enough to evict Houston from his office on March 16, 1861, for refusing to take an oath of loyalty to the Confederacy, which Texas had joined on March 2. Houston wrote:

> *Fellow-Citizens, in the name of your rights and liberties, which I believe have been trampled upon…In the name of the nationality of Texas, which has been betrayed by the Convention…In the name of my own conscience and manhood, which this Convention would degrade by dragging me before it, to pander to the malice of my enemies, I refuse to take this oath…I protest against all the acts and doings of this convention and I declare them null and void.*

He was replaced by Lieutenant Governor Edward Clark. To avoid more bloodshed in Texas, Houston turned down U.S. colonel Frederick W. Lander's offer from President Lincoln of fifty thousand troops to prevent Texas's secession. After leaving the governor's mansion, Houston traveled to Galveston. Along the way, many people demanded an explanation for his refusal to support the Confederacy. On April 19, 1861, from a hotel window, he told a crowd:

> *Let me tell you what is coming. After the sacrifice of countless millions of treasure and hundreds of thousands of lives, you may win Southern independence if God be not against you, but I doubt it. I tell you that, while I believe with you in the doctrine of states' rights, the North is determined to preserve this Union. They are not a fiery, impulsive people as you are, for they live in colder climates. But when they begin to move in a given direction, they move with the steady momentum and perseverance of a mighty avalanche; and what I fear is, they will overwhelm the South.*

What follows is an excerpt from the Texas Ordinance of Secession:

> *AN ORDINANCE to dissolve the Union between the State of Texas and the other States united under the Compact styled "the Constitution of the United States of America."*
>
> *SECTION 1. We, the people of the State of Texas, by delegates in convention assembled, do declare and ordain that the ordinance adopted by our convention of delegates on the 4th day of July, A.D. 1845, under which the Republic of Texas was admitted into the Union with other States, and became a party to the compact styled "The Constitution of the United States of America," be, and is hereby, repealed and annulled; that all the powers which, by the said compact, were delegated by Texas to the Federal Government are revoked and resumed;…and that her citizens and people are absolved from all allegiance to the United States or the government thereof…*

I have given here just parts of each state's Articles of Secession. Each one deals with states' rights and the North's interference with private property, meaning the slavery issue. Meanwhile, on February 13, the Virginia Secession Convention assembled in Richmond. Having been called for by a special session of the General Assembly, the group convened to determine whether Virginia should secede from the Union.

The first national flag of the Confederacy, also known as the Stars and Bars. It contained seven stars for the seven Deep South states that left the Union.

On November 15, 1860, Virginia governor John Letcher had called for a special session of the Virginia General Assembly to consider, among other issues, the creation of a secession convention. The legislature convened on January 7 and approved the convention on January 14. On January 19, the General Assembly called for a national peace convention, led by Virginia's former U.S. president John Tyler, to be held in Washington City on February 4, the same date that elections were scheduled for delegates to the secession convention.

The election of secession convention delegates drew 152 representatives. Thirty of these delegates were strong secessionists, 30 were equally strong unionists and 92 were moderates who were not clearly identified with either of the first two groups. Nevertheless, advocates of immediate secession were clearly outnumbered. Simultaneous to this election, six Southern states formed the Confederate States of America on February 4.

The Virginia Secession Convention met on February 13 at the Richmond Mechanics Institute. John Janney of Loudoun County, a unionist, onetime potential vice-presidential candidate (and almost president—John Tyler had beaten him out as vice president on William Henry Harrison's ticket in 1840) and well-respected lawyer, was named president of the convention. Eppa Hunton, commonwealth's attorney from Prince William County, was the only Northern Virginian who favored secession during the first vote. In his *Autobiography*, Hunton wrote:

> *I took the ground that I was for immediate secession for the sake of the Union. I argued that if Virginia would go out of the Union, at once, followed by some of the border states, the movement would be so formidable that the U.S. Government would not make war upon the Confederate States, but that the doctrine which was held by a great many Northern people, to* Let the erring sisters go in peace, *would be adopted even by the Lincoln Administration. When war was avoided, reconstruction would take place between the North and the South on terms satisfactory to both sides and permanent.*

As the Peace Convention dragged on, former president John Tyler also began toying with the idea of secession. He believed that if Virginia seceded, the rest of the Border States and even a few Northern states would depart from the Union, leaving a weakened North that would not feel itself strong enough militarily to crush so powerful a Confederacy.

One of the secession convention's first actions was to create a twenty-one-member Federal Relations Committee charged with reaching a compromise to the sectional differences as they affected Virginia. The committee was made up of four secessionists, ten moderates and seven unionists. At first there was no urgency to the convention's deliberations as all sides felt that time only aided their causes. In addition, there were hopes that the Peace Convention, led by John Tyler, might resolve the crisis. With the failure of the Peace Convention at the end of February, moderates in the convention began to waver in their support for unionism. Unionist support was further eroded for many Virginians by Lincoln's March 4 first inaugural address, which they felt was argumentative if not defiant. Throughout the state, there was evidence that support for secession was growing.

John Janney. This Unionist from Loudoun County was elected president of the Virginia Secession Convention.

2

Virginia Secedes and
Her Favorite Son Follows

The Federal Relations Committee made its report to the secession convention on March 9. The fourteen proposals defended both slavery and states' rights while calling for a meeting of the eight slave states (Virginia, North Carolina, Tennessee, Arkansas, Maryland, Kentucky, Missouri and Delaware) still in the Union to present a united front for compromise—and possibly setting up a buffer Union of Border States between the Deep South and the North. From March 15 through April 14, the convention debated these proposals one by one. During the debate on the resolutions, the sixth resolution calling for a peaceful solution and maintenance of the Union came up for discussion on April 4. Lewis Edwin Harvie of Amelia County offered a substitute resolution calling for immediate secession. This was voted down, eighty-eight to forty-five, and the next day the convention continued its debate. Approval of the last proposal came on April 12. The goal of the unionist faction after this approval was to adjourn the convention until October, allowing time for both the convention of the slave states and Virginia's congressional elections in May, which, it hoped, would produce a stronger mandate for compromise.

At the same time, unionists were concerned about the continued presence of federal forces at Fort Sumter in Charleston Harbor, South Carolina, despite assurances communicated informally to them by U.S. secretary of state William Seward that it would be abandoned. Lincoln and Seward were also concerned that the Virginia convention was still in session as of the first of April while secession sentiment was growing. At Lincoln's invitation, unionist John B. Baldwin of Augusta County met with Lincoln on April 4. Baldwin explained that the unionists needed the evacuation of Fort Sumter, a national convention to debate the sectional differences and a commitment by Lincoln to support constitutional protections for Southern rights. Over Lincoln's skepticism, Baldwin argued that Virginia would be out of the Union within forty-eight hours if either side fired a shot at the fort. By some accounts, Lincoln offered to evacuate Fort Sumter if the Virginia convention would adjourn.

On April 6, amid rumors that the North was preparing for war, the convention voted by a narrow 63–57 to send a three-man delegation to Washington City to determine from Lincoln what his intentions were. However, due to bad weather, the delegation did not arrive in Washington City until April 12. They learned of the attack on Fort Sumter from Lincoln, and the president advised them of his intent to hold the fort and respond to force with force. Reading from a prepared text to prevent any misinterpretations of his intent, Lincoln told them that he had made it clear in his inaugural address that the forts and arsenals in the South were government property, and "if...an unprovoked assault has been made upon Fort Sumter, I shall hold myself at liberty to re-possess, if I can, like places which have been seized before the Government was devolved upon me."

Any pro-Union sentiment in Virginia was further weakened after the Confederate attack on Fort Sumter. Richmond reacted with large public demonstrations in support of the Confederacy on April 13, when it first received the news of the attack. The convention reconvened on April 13 to reconsider Virginia's position, given the outbreak of hostilities. With Virginia still in a delicate balance, with no firm determination yet to secede, sentiment turned more strongly toward secession on April 15, following President Lincoln's call to all states that had not declared secession, including Virginia, for seventy-five thousand troops to assist in halting the insurrection and recovering the captured forts.

The quota for Virginia called for three regiments of 2,340 men to rendezvous at Staunton, Wheeling and Gordonsville. Governor Letcher and the recently reconvened Virginia Secession Convention considered this request from Lincoln "for troops to invade and coerce" lacking in constitutional authority and out of scope of the Act of 1795. Governor Letcher's reply was that the call made an immediate change in the public opinion in Virginia.

Lithograph of the bombardment of Fort Sumter in Charleston Harbor. This act and President Lincoln's calling up of seventy-five thousand volunteers to quell the rebellion pushed Virginia into the secessionist camp. *Courtesy of Douglas Bostick.*

Thereafter, the secession convention voted eighty-eight to fifty-five on April 17, provisionally, to secede on the condition of ratification by a statewide referendum.

An Ordinance

To Repeal the ratification of the Constitution of the United States of America, by the State of Virginia, and to resume all the rights and powers granted under said Constitution:

The people of Virginia, in their ratification of the Constitution of the United States of America, adopted by them in Convention, on the 25th day of June, in the year of our Lord one thousand seven hundred and eighty-eight, having declared that the powers granted them under the said Constitution were derived from the people of the United States, and might be resumed whensoever the same should be perverted to their injury and oppression, and the Federal Government having perverted said powers, not only to the injury of the people of Virginia, but to the oppression of the Southern slaveholding States.

Now, therefore, we, the people of Virginia, do declare and ordain that the Ordinance adopted by the people of this State in Convention, on the twenty-fifth day of June, in the year of our Lord one thousand seven hundred and eighty-eight, whereby the Constitution of the United States of America was ratified, and all acts of the General Assembly of this State, ratifying or adopting amendments to said Constitution, are hereby repealed and abrogated; that the union between the State of Virginia and the other States under the Constitution aforesaid, is hereby dissolved, and that the State of Virginia is in the full possession and exercise of all the rights of sovereignty which belong to a free and independent State. And they do further declare that the said Constitution of the United State of America is no longer binding on any of the citizens of this State.

This Ordinance shall take effect and be an act of this day when ratified by a majority of the votes of the people of this State, cast at a poll to be taken thereon on the fourth Thursday in May next, in pursuance of a schedule hereafter to be enacted.

Done in Convention, in the city of Richmond, on the seventeenth day of April, in the year of our Lord one thousand eight hundred and sixty-one, and in the eighty-fifth year of the Commonwealth of Virginia.

Governor Letcher immediately began mobilizing the Virginia State Militia to strategic points around the state. Former governor Henry Wise had arranged with militia officers on April 16, before the final vote, to seize the U.S. arsenal at Harpers Ferry and the Gosport Navy Yard in Norfolk. On April 17, in the debate over secession, Wise announced to the convention that these events were already in motion. On April 18, the arsenal was captured, and most of the machinery was moved to Richmond. At Gosport, the Union navy, fooled into believing that several thousand militiamen were headed their way, evacuated and abandoned Norfolk and the navy yard, burning and torching as many of the ships and facilities as possible.

Northern Virginia's most famous and sought-after resident, Colonel Robert E. Lee, resigned his U.S. Army commission on April 20, turning down an offer of command for the U.S. Army. Lee's father, "Light Horse Harry" Lee, had been one of George Washington's cavalry commanders during the Revolutionary War and, upon Washington's death, uttered the immortal words: "First in war, first in peace, first in the hearts of his countrymen." Lee's wife, Mary, was the only surviving child of George Washington Parke Custis, grandson of Martha Washington and adopted son of George Washington. Mr. Custis had started building his mansion on his eleven-hundred-acre estate in 1802, following the death of Martha and three years after the death of George Washington. Custis originally wanted to name the property Mount Washington but was persuaded by family members to name it Arlington House after the Custis family's homestead on the Eastern Shore of Virginia.

The young Robert E. Lee, whose mother was a cousin of Mrs. Custis, frequently visited Arlington and knew Mary growing up. Two years after graduating from West Point, Lieutenant Lee married Mary Anna Custis at Arlington on June 30, 1831. For thirty years Arlington House was home to the Lees. They spent much of their married life traveling between U.S. Army duty stations and Arlington, where six of their seven children were born. They shared this home with Mary's parents, the Custises, until her parents died; they are buried on the grounds.

Upon George Washington Parke Custis's death in 1857, he left the Arlington estate to Mary Custis Lee for her lifetime and thence to the Lees' eldest son, George Washington Custis Lee. Robert E. Lee was never an owner of the property. The estate needed much repair and reorganization, and Lieutenant Colonel Lee, as executor of Custis's complicated will, took a leave of absence from the army until 1860 to begin the necessary agricultural and financial improvements.

It was during his stay at Arlington that Lee had been called upon by the U.S. government to put down the slave revolt, led by John Brown, in Harpers

Arlington House, built in the early nineteenth century by George Washington Parke Custis, adopted son of George Washington and father-in-law of Robert E. Lee. *Courtesy of Douglas Bostick.*

Ferry in October 1859. This event is sometimes considered the opening salvo of the Civil War. After his capture, Brown proclaimed, "You people had better prepare yourselves for the settlement of that question—this negro question, I mean. You think you have gotten rid of me easily enough I know, I am almost disposed now; but this question is still to be settled, the end of this is not yet. More John Browns will come soon enough." Brown was hanged for treason in December 1859.

In February 1860, Lee was ordered to return to Texas, where he had been performing his army duties since 1855. He was there for the entire year, until he was called back to Washington City in February 1861. In January, he had written to his eldest son, Custis:

> *The South, in my opinion, has been aggrieved by the acts of the North, as you say. I feel the aggression, and am willing to take every proper step for redress. It is the principle I contend for, not individual or private gain. As an American citizen, I take great pride in my country, her prosperity and institutions, and would defend any State if her rights were invaded. But I can anticipate no greater calamity for the country than dissolution of the Union. It would be an accumulation of all the*

evils we complain of, and I am willing to sacrifice everything but honor for its preservation. I hope therefore, that all constitutional means will be exhausted before there is recourse to force. Secession is nothing but revolution. The framers of our Constitution never exhausted so much labor, wisdom and forbearance in its formation, and surrounded it with so many guards and securities, if it was intended to be broken by every member of the Confederacy at will. It was intended for "perpetual union" so expressed in the preamble, and for the establishment of a government, not a compact, which can only be dissolved by revolution, or the consent of all the people in convention assembled. It is idle to talk of secession. Anarchy would have been established, and not a government by Washington, Hamilton, Jefferson, Madison, and the other patriots of the Revolution. Still, a Union that can only be maintained by swords and bayonets, and in which strife and civil war are to take the place of brotherly love and kindness, has no charm for me. I shall mourn for my country and for the welfare and progress of mankind. If the Union is dissolved, and the Government disrupted, I shall return to my native State and share the miseries of my people, and save in defence will draw my sword on none.

By discretion and silence he avoided a commitment that might have had a momentous effect on his own career and on the whole course of the war. For what might have happened if he had been in command of the Department of Texas instead of General David E. Twiggs when the Texans demanded surrender of Federal property that February? Twiggs had replaced Lee as commander in December 1860. Twiggs, originally from Georgia and a proponent of states' rights, surrendered all U.S. Army arms and property to the Texas secessionists. Twiggs subsequently was dismissed from the U.S. Army for "treachery to the flag of his country" and accepted a commission as a major general from the Confederate States. Lee's own state of Virginia had not seceded; he would have had no hesitancy in obeying the orders of the War Department and would have refused to surrender government property. Would he then have clashed with the Texans? Would he have been the first to face secession fire? Very nearly the Civil War began in February in Texas instead of in April in South Carolina, with Lieutenant Colonel Robert E. Lee playing the part of Major Robert Anderson.

As speedily as he could, Lee prepared to leave San Antonio. When friends came to say goodbye, his views were freely expressed and fully understood.

To one officer, he said simply and in the deepest distress, "When I get to Virginia I think the world will have one soldier less. I shall resign and go to planting corn."

Shortly after his arrival back in Washington City, early in March, Lee met with General Winfield Scott at the War Department. For three hours, the old general and his favorite subordinate talked together. What they said was never revealed. But Scott's known opinion against secession, even though he was from Virginia, his admiration for Lee and his desire to ensure good leadership for the army make it possible to reconstruct the substance of at least part of what was said. Scott probably told Lee that he was soon to be made a colonel, and then he hinted that if he (Scott) found himself too feeble to take the field, he would recommend Lee as his second in command. Scott would deliberately have sought to appeal to Lee's ambitions, but knowing Lee as he did, Scott did not try to buy his allegiance with promises, which, indeed, Scott was not authorized to make. If Lee replied to Scott's overtures, it was to say that if Virginia seceded, he would follow her course because he considered his first obligation to be to her. Scott, of course, was of a temper to argue this and probably ended a lengthy oration with the request that Lee go home, think the subject over and await further developments. When Lee left, it was reported that Scott's manner was "painfully silent."

About the same time, Lee got a letter from LeRoy Pope Walker, Confederate secretary of war, written on March 15. This was a direct offer of a commission as brigadier general, the highest rank then authorized, in the army the South was raising. "You are requested," the letter read, "to signify your acceptance or non-acceptance of said appointment, and should you accept you will sign before a magistrate the oath of office herewith and forward the same, with your letter of acceptance to this office." After the long years of slow promotion, the honors were coming fast—a colonelcy in one army and a like offer of a generalship in the rival service. There is no record of any reply by Lee to this tender from the new Confederacy. It is probable that he ignored the offer, and it is certain that he was not lured by the promise of high position. He owed allegiance to only two governments, that of Virginia and that of the Union, and there could be no thought of a third so long as these two did not conflict and Virginia did not throw in her destiny with the Confederate States.

By March 28, Lee had been promoted to full colonel in the U.S. Army and had taken the oath of allegiance to the U.S. Constitution. On the morning of April 18, with no news from the Virginia Secession Convention in Richmond, Lee rode over the bridge and up to see Francis Preston Blair

Colonel Robert E. Lee, as he would have appeared at his resignation from the U.S. Army in April 1861. *Courtesy of Douglas Bostick.*

in his house, across the street from the presidential mansion. Blair and Lee were distantly related by marriage. Originally a Democrat, Blair was now a power in the Republican Party. They sat down behind closed doors. Blair promptly and plainly explained his reason for asking Lee to call. A large army, he said, was soon to be called into the field to enforce Federal law; President Lincoln had authorized him to ask Lee if he would accept the command.

Command of an army of 75,000, perhaps 100,000 men; opportunity to apply all he had learned in Mexico; the supreme ambition of a soldier realized; the full support of the government; many of his ablest comrades working with him; rank as a major general—all this was put before Lee. Lee responded, "If the Union is dissolved and the government disrupted, I shall return to my native state and share the miseries of my people and save in her defence will draw my sword on no one." There he made the fateful reply he later recalled in an account of the interview: "I declined the offer he made me to take command of the army that was to be brought into the field, stating as candidly and as courteously as I could, that though opposed to secession and deprecating war, I could take no part in an invasion of the Southern States." That was all, as far as Lee was concerned. He had long before decided, instinctively, what his duty required of him, and the allure of supreme command, with all that a soldier craved, did not tempt him to equivocate for an instant or to see if there were not some way he could keep his own honor and still have the honor he understood the president had offered him. Blair talked on in a futile hope of converting Lee, but it was to no purpose.

Bidding farewell to Blair, Lee went directly to General Scott's office. He sensed Scott's deep interest in his action, and as soon as he had arrived, he told him what Blair had offered and what he had answered. "Lee," said Scott, deeply moved, "you have made the greatest mistake of your life; but

I feared it would be so." Deep as was the difference between the two men on a public question that made personal enemies of many lifelong friends, Scott did not stop with this sad observation but expressed the belief that if Lee were going to resign, he ought not to delay. "There are times," Scott is reported to have said, "when every officer in the United States service should fully determine what course he will pursue and frankly declare it. No one should continue in government employ without being actively employed." And again he added, "I suppose you will go with the rest. If you purpose to resign, it is proper that you should do so at once; your present attitude is equivocal."

At length, over the route he had so often traveled, Lee rode out of Washington City, across the bridge and up the quiet hills to the home whose white columns he could see for most of the way. He was never again to make that journey in that same fashion.

The next morning, April 19, Lee went into Alexandria on business, and there he read the news he had hoped he would never see: Virginia had seceded. To his mind, that meant the wreck of the nation, "the beginning of sorrows," the opening of a war that was certain to be long and full of horrors. But of all that he thought and felt in the first realization that his mother state had left the Union, his only recorded observation is one he made to a druggist when he went into a shop to a pay a bill. "I must say," he remarked sadly, as a comment on the celebrations going on in the city, "that I am one of those dull creatures that cannot see the good of secession."

If Lee had any doubt of the truth of the report in the Alexandria paper that morning, it was soon removed. That afternoon, the *Washington Star* took the news for granted. By nightfall on the nineteenth, Lee had no alternative to believing it. When other hopes had failed him before this time, Lee had told himself that secession could not become an accomplished fact until the voters of Virginia had passed on the ordinance of secession, as they had specifically reserved the right to do, but now Lee's judgment told him that war would not wait on a referendum. Virginia would certainly consider that her safety required the seizure of Federal depots within her borders. Had not Texas similarly provided for a referendum on secession, and had not he, with his own eyes, seen how the Texas committee of safety had committed an act of war by seizing U.S. property without waiting for the people to confirm or disavow the ordinance of the convention?

The Federal government, for its part, would certainly take prompt action since the state just across the river from its capital had left the Union. As one of the senior field officers in Washington City, Lee might be summoned at any hour to defend Washington City by invading Virginia—which he could not do. His duty was plain. There could be no holding back. The time had come. All the Lees had been Americans, but they had been Virginians first. His own father, "Light Horse Harry" called Virginia "my native country." Now revolution and the older allegiance were the same. The son must be as Washington, his great model, who had embraced a revolutionary cause. Dearly as Lee loved the Union, anxious as he was to see it preserved, he could not bear arms against the South. Virginia had seceded and doubtless would join the South; her action controlled his, and he could not wait for the uncertain vote of the people when war was upon him. So after midnight, as the nineteenth became the twentieth, he sat down and wrote a letter of resignation to Simon Cameron, U.S. secretary of war, not more than fifteen hours after he had received positive information that Virginia had seceded:

> *I have the honor to tender the resignation of my commission as Colonel of the 1ˢᵗ Regt. of Cavalry.*
> *Very resp'y Your Obedient Servant.*
> *R.E. Lee*
> *Col 1ˢᵗ Cav'y.*

Lee also wrote to General Scott:

> *Since my interview with you on the 18ᵗʰ inst. I have felt that I ought no longer to retain my commission in the Army. I therefore tender my resignation, which I request you will recommend for acceptance. I would have presented it at once, but for the struggle it has cost me to separate myself from a service to which I have devoted all the best years of my life and all the ability I possessed.*
>
> *During the whole of that time—more than a quarter of a century—I have experienced nothing but kindness from my superiors and a most cordial friendship from my comrades. To no one, General, have I been as much indebted as to yourself for uniform kindness and consideration, and it has always been my ardent desire to meet your approbation. I shall carry to the grave the most grateful recollections of your kind consideration, and your name and fame will always be dear to me.*
>
> *Save in defence of my native State, I never desire again to draw my sword.*
>
> *Be pleased to accept my most earnest wishes for the continuance of your happiness and prosperity, and believe me, most truly yours,*
> *R.E. Lee.*

Virginia Secedes and Her Favorite Son Follows

When he took up his daily paper, the *Alexandria Gazette*, it was to discover that others were interested in the action he had taken, for an editorial article read as follows:

> *It is probable that the secession of Virginia will cause an immediate resignation of many officers of the Army and Navy from this State. We do not know, and have no right to speak for or anticipate the course of Colonel Robert E. Lee. Whatever he may do, will be conscientious and honorable. But if he should resign his present position in the U.S. Army, we call the immediate attention of our State to him, as an able, brave, experienced officer—no man his superior in all that constitutes the soldier and the gentleman—no man more worthy to head our forces and lead our army. There is no man who would command more of the confidence of the people of Virginia, than this distinguished officer; and no one under whom the volunteers and militia would more gladly rally. His reputation, his acknowledged ability, his chivalric character, his probity, honor, and—may we add, to his eternal praise—his Christian life and conduct—make his very name a tower of strength. It is a name surrounded by revolutionary and patriotic associations and reminiscences.*

It was not a pleasant article for a modest man to read, and it was disquieting, besides, with its assurance that some, at least, were looking to him to lead the army of Virginia against the Union and the old flag if war came. He could only pray it would not. Late in the evening, Lee received a letter from Judge John Robertson of Richmond. The judge was then in Alexandria and asked for an interview the next day. Lee set 1:00 p.m. as the hour and offered to meet the judge in town.

On Sunday morning, April 21, dressed in civilian clothes, Lee went into Alexandria with one of his daughters to attend service at Christ Church. The town was wild with excitement. Overwhelmingly Southern in their sentiment, the people rejoiced at the secession of Virginia as if it meant deliverance from bondage. In their enthusiasm, they fancied they were repeating the drama of 1776 and that the spirit of Washington gave its benediction to a new revolution. In all this rejoicing, Lee took no part. His resignation was not generally known as yet, though his neighbors and friends had been waiting to see what he would do. His sorrow, his sense of the fitness of things and his knowledge that war would be long and terrible kept him from any statement of his action.

A thirty-three-star U.S. flag. The same banner flew over Fort Sumter during its bombardment in April 1861.

Afterward, Lee engaged in serious conversation with three men who were unknown to the congregation and whose identities have never been established. His neighbors and friends thought the strangers were commissioners from the governor of Virginia, but it seems more probable that they were companions of Judge Robertson, who explained that the judge had gone to Washington City and had been detained there but would soon arrive to keep his appointment. Lee had not been in communication with the state convention or with the governor. He had no information as to the military plans. Perhaps the visitors acquainted him with what had happened and intimated that his service was desired by his mother state, but in Judge Robertson's absence there could have been nothing official. Lee waited and chatted for several hours and then, concluding that Robertson would not return, rode back to Arlington.

That evening, a messenger arrived at the mansion with a letter from Robertson. He apologized for his delay and invited Lee, in the name of the governor, to repair to Richmond for a conference with the chief executive. Lee realized, of course, that this meant participation in the defense of Virginia, but he did not hesitate an hour. The very reason that had impelled him to resign from the U.S. army—his allegiance to Virginia—prompted him to sit down at once and write an answer to Robertson. Virginia's action in withdrawing from the Union carried him with her, and if she called him now, it was his duty to obey. In a few words, he notified the governor's representative that he would join him in Alexandria the next day, in time to take the train for Richmond. There was no questioning, no holding back, no delay. But Lee never regretted his action, never even admitted that he had made a choice. After the war, he said, "I did only what my duty demanded. I could have taken no other course without dishonor. And if it all were to be done over again, I should act in precisely the same manner."

Lee reported to Richmond for the duty of commanding Virginia's Provisional Army. He joined the Confederate States Army with Virginia's forces a month later and was promoted to general. Lee was concerned for the safety of his wife, who was still residing at the mansion, and convinced her to vacate the property.

She managed to send many of the family's valuables off to safety, as she had advance notice of the impending Union occupation from her cousin, Orton W. Williams. Lieutenant Williams was on Scott's staff. Mary Custis Lee left the property in mid-May, going out to her cousins' twenty-two-thousand-acre estate at Ravensworth in Fairfax County. Robert E. Lee never set foot on the property again, but shortly before her 1873 death, Mary Lee visited Arlington once more. Arlington was captured as part of the Union advance into Northern Virginia on the morning of May 24, the day after the voters ratified the Articles of Secession.

On May 6, Arkansas seceded:

> AN ORDINANCE to dissolve the union now existing between the State of Arkansas and the other States united with her under the compact entitled "The Constitution of the United States of America."
>
> Whereas, in addition to the well-founded causes of complaint set forth by this convention, in resolutions adopted on the 11th of March, A.D. 1861, against the sectional party now in power in Washington City, headed by Abraham Lincoln, he has, in the face of resolutions passed by this convention pledging the State of Arkansas to resist to the last extremity any attempt on the part of such power to coerce any State that had seceded from the old Union, proclaimed to the world that war should be waged against such States until they should be compelled to submit to their rule, and large forces to accomplish this have by this same power been called out, and are now being marshaled to carry out this inhuman design; and to longer submit to such rule, or remain in the old Union of the United States, would be disgraceful and ruinous to the State of Arkansas.

On May 20, North Carolina seceded:

> AN ORDINANCE to dissolve the union between the State of North Carolina and the other States united with her, under the compact of government entitled "The Constitution of the United States."
>
> We, the people of the State of North Carolina in convention assembled, do declare and ordain, That the ordinance adopted by the State of North

Carolina in the convention of 1789, whereby the Constitution of the United States was ratified and adopted, and also all acts and parts of acts of the General Assembly ratifying and adopting amendments to the said Constitution, are hereby repealed, rescinded, and abrogated.

We do further declare and ordain, That the union now subsisting between the State of North Carolina and the other States, under the title of the United States of America, is hereby dissolved, and that the State of North Carolina is in full possession and exercise of all those rights of sovereignty which belong and appertain to a free and independent State.

Done in convention at the city of Raleigh, this 20th day of May, in the year of our Lord 1861, and in the eighty-fifth year of the independence of said State.

3

Alexandria County Is
Liberated/Invaded

From April 20 until May 23, the city of Alexandria existed in a state of suspended animation. The original unbridled joy over the secession of the state gradually gave way to a sense of foreboding over its neighbor across the Potomac, Washington City, now the capital of the foreign United States of America. From mid-May, the U.S. warship *Pawnee* was stationed menacingly off the harbor. Even though a statewide vote on secession would not be held until May 23, Virginia was already acting as a separate entity from the United States. As the voting progressed on May 23, it became clear that the voters (at that time, free white men twenty-one and older) were following the lead of their representatives in leaving the Union.

The following are the remembrances of a citizen of Alexandria, A.J. Wickliffe, written in 1889, about the events of May 24, 1861:

> *Early in the morning of May 24, 1861, before the citizens were out of their beds, the Union army commenced pouring in from all quarters, over bridges and by steamers. The atmosphere seemed to be full of them.*
>
> *The New York Zouaves, under command of Col. Ellsworth* [Elmer E. Ellsworth (b. 1837; d. 1861)] *landed from a steamer at the foot of Cameron Street. They marched up that street, the head of the column resting under my window. I looked down and saw Colonel Ellsworth detail a squad from the ranks, and, at the head of it, made for the Marshall House on King Street, kept by a Mr. Jackson* [James W. Jackson (b.1823; d.1861)]. *Upon the top floated a large Confederate flag. Upon reaching the*

The USS *Pawnee*. This warship first patrolled near Alexandria, Virginia, and then landed Colonel Ellsworth and his Zouaves in the early morning of May 24, 1861.

building, Col. Ellsworth, at the head of the column, made his way to the top of the building, hauling down the flag and wrapping it around his body. In retracing his steps he had to pass Jackson's chamber door. In doing so, Jackson stepped out of his room with a double barrel shot gun, and fired at the man who had his flag around him. Ellsworth fell dead instantly [shot through the heart], and the guards fired on Jackson. He fell, rolled to the landing below, was pierced many times with bayonets, and left for dead.

Jackson was a brave man. The writer knew him well. I have often heard him say that he would shoot any man who attempted to haul his flag down, and true to his word died in the defence of the flag he loved so well. He had received repeated messages from the Union forces, that his flag would be their first capture; it could be plainly seen from the White House and was to be presented to Mr. Lincoln. This was the first blood shed in the great civil war that followed, and had its effect in intensifying and aggravating the already bitter feeling that existed. Col. Ellsworth's body was placed on a stretcher, and borne by four of his soldiers to the boat [USS Pawnee], and taken to Washington.

The excitement over these tragic events, I can never forget. The citizens felt they had little or no security; the soldiers made open threats of sacking the city. We were now amid the "pomp and circumstance" of war; preparations were rapidly pushed forward to organize and equip the armies for the capture of the "rebel" stronghold in Manassas. It was very generally *known by the citizens—the time fixed for the advance of the armies. The constant arrival of troops, batteries of artillery innumerable, all pointed to the fact that the great conflict was near at hand. Methought I saw enough soldiers pass through and around Alexandria to whip every soldier of every nation on earth combined.*

The owner of the Marshall House, James W. Jackson, was the same person who had chopped down the Liberty Pole in Occoquan the previous July. Here in Alexandria, Jackson killed Colonel Ellsworth and died himself, trying to protect his freedom of political expression, the same freedom he had so easily denied others in 1860. Such an example of irony would be difficult to find elsewhere. Two men died: one Union, one Confederate. Both became martyrs and heroes to their causes.

Photo of the Marshall House, with Union troops out front. *Courtesy of the Library of Congress.*

Sisters Anne and Lizzie Frobel were living just south of Alexandria at Wilton Hill (near the present intersection of Telegraph Road and Franconia Road). On May 25, Anne determined to keep a diary to record the events resulting from Northern troops taking control of Alexandria and the surrounding areas. Here is what she wrote a few days after May 24:

Lizzie having gone on an errand to a neighbors I was left entirely alone sitting in the living room at work, when in walked three officers (horrible creatures), dressed up in all their trappings, pistols stuck in their belts, and swords clanging against the floor—I was frightened almost out of my wits. I never asked them in or to be seated. I never said a word. I don't believe I could speak if I had tried. I did not know what was coming I expected to be annihilated. Two of them stationed themselves on either side of the fireplace and held up the mantel piece with their shoulders the other one strutted up to me and said we have come to search this house. He turned and walked across the room to the side-board pulled open one of the drawers.

At this time, one of our neighbors came in, looked in the door perfectly aghast with her mouth open and darted up stairs. Mr. Lieu. Searcher after opening the drawers and turning over the table cloth and napkins and things that were in it turned to me and said "this is a very disagreeable business." I stood up all the time as straight as a line, by this time I was too indignant to feel afraid of them, and replied, "I should think so and not only disagreeable but very degrading." The man let go the drawers and dropped back into a seat as if I had shot him, said "I assure you any search is only for fire-arms." I replied, ladies have very little use for fire-arms, and as my sister and myself were the only white people living in this house you could hardly expect to find anything of the kind here. "O" he said, "You are the ladies I have heard of, if I had known it I would not have disturbed you"…

The next day another party came with their bright gleaming guns and bayonets stuck on the ends, (fixed I believe they call it) and demanded something to eat, which was given to them, and the next day they came and the next—and the next and every day, morning, noon and night always the same tune something to eat, until it was enough to run one crazy and they nearly eaten up all we have, all the roads in and about town are picketed and they will not allow us to bring any thing from there so that with our own family and these horrible yankee germands we are getting rather scarce of provisions.

Miss Anne had the following ruminations on the Zouaves and the events in the area near and in Alexandria:

O the horrible, horrible red legs—the fire Zouaves—here they come again with their tight blue skull caps and long chords and tassels hanging from the top-knot I think it possible they are more savage than the rest they are our perfect terror. Their red clothes can be seen from afar. They are the New York City fire Zouaves—The soldiers seem to have no particular uniform. Each company seems to be caprisoned according to their own peculiar style and fancy. They came here dressed in all manner of frippery, some in dark clothes with broad brimmed hats and long black plumes, others in gray with tight caps with a long fox tail stuck straight up in front and O the Fox Tails are a vile set! They searched Mr. Reid's house recently and found a Confederate flag, and then such vile doings never anyone heard of before, they tore the whole house and place up generally. They manacled him and dragged him off to town through all the water and mud-holes they could find—and up and down through every street until he was wearied and worn almost to death, and then put him in prison where they kept him until he was forced to take the oath (whatever that is).

Today is the first time we have ventured to leave home since the invasion. Some pickets were stationed about on the roads but they did not interfere with us, but it was dreadful to see the destruction all about, fields thrown open, fences all down, fires all burning in the fields piled up with rails, grain fields that so short a time ago were looking so beautiful and flourishing, now covered over with tents, and trampled over with horses, and wagons, and soldiers and every thing pertaining to an army. The streets were also filled with them, and so shockingly filthy that it made me shudder to walk on the pavements. And every body looking so sad and sorrowful, and all having a tale of horror and wrong to tell.

MILITARY PREPARATIONS IN NORTHERN VIRGINIA

Northern Virginians had been preparing for any war-like contingencies since before 1861. The core of the Seventeenth Virginia Infantry, Confederate States Army (CSA), organized at Manassas Junction on June 10, 1861, had marched out of Alexandria as Northern troops were coming in on May 24. It was composed of ten companies, many of which began as prewar

Statue of "Appomattox" (with inset of base) in Old Town Alexandria, Virginia. From this point, Southern-sympathetic troops departed from Alexandria to join Confederate forces near Manassas.

volunteer militias. The volunteers were from Alexandria, Fairfax, Fauquier, Loudoun, Prince William and Warren Counties.

The foundation of these volunteers was four companies organized on February 18, 1861, as a volunteer militia battalion. The Mount Vernon Guard, Alexandria Riflemen, Old Dominion Rifles and Alexandria Artillery were attached to the 175th Regiment (Alexandria County), Virginia Militia. On April 2, the General Assembly passed an act authorizing a battalion to be raised in the city of Alexandria with three companies of infantry and one of artillery. On April 4, Captain Montgomery Dent Corse, of the Old Dominion Rifles, was unanimously elected to command the battalion as a major.

The oldest company, the Mount Vernon Guard, was organized on June 21, 1842, but always observed July 4 as its anniversary. The first time the men probably appeared in uniform was in October 1842, when they passed in review before President John Tyler. The Alexandria Riflemen were organized on March 10, 1856. Originally choosing the name Alexandria

Sharp Shooters, they quickly reconvened their meeting when some realized how the initials would look painted on the back of their knapsacks. The change of name to Alexandria Riflemen was unanimous. They were organized, with the Mount Vernon Guard, into a volunteer battalion under the command of Major Turner Wade Ashby. Ashby had been a lieutenant in Captain Corse's company during the Mexican War.

The Old Dominion Rifles was organized on December 6, 1860. Organization was complete by January 7, 1861, with the election of Corse as captain and Arthur Herbert as lieutenant. Mr. Herbert, together with John W. Burke, had formed Burke and Herbert Bank in Alexandria in 1852. The Alexandria Artillery was formed in 1850 as the Mechanical Artillery. The new name was adopted in 1856. Two companies of the Irish citizens of Alexandria were added to the battalion on April 25, 1861—an artillery company, the Irish Volunteers, and a light infantry company, the Emmett Guards. Two Fairfax County cavalry companies joined the battalion, as well: the Chesterfield Troop and the Fairfax Cavalry, known also as the Washington Home Guard.

Before the end of April, three more companies were attached to Corse's command at Alexandria. On April 24, the eighty men of the Loudoun Guard arrived from Leesburg. This light infantry company was organized early in November 1859 by Captain Charles B. Tebbs. It was attached to the Fifty-seventh Regiment (Loudoun County), Virginia Militia.

The Fairfax Rifles had been formed at Fairfax Court House by Captain William H. Dulany on December 1, 1859, as the Fairfax Rifle Rangers and attached to the Sixtieth Regiment (Fairfax County), Virginia Militia. James W. Jackson was an early member of the Sixtieth Militia before moving to Alexandria to become proprietor of the Marshall House. The Fairfax Rifles joined Corse under the command of Lieutenant William A. Barnes on April 25, 1861, and were assigned to barracks on Prince Street, near Fairfax Street.

Captain Robert H. Simpson, a teacher and Virginia Military Institute graduate, organized the Warren Rifles in Front Royal (Warren County). The company marched to Winchester on April 18, 1861, to enroll for active service. From there, it proceeded by rail to Harpers Ferry. Ordered to Alexandria to escort a shipment of captured arms, the men stopped at Front Royal and arrived in Alexandria on April 26. By April 27, Corse's command was designated as the Sixth Battalion of Virginia Volunteers under Lieutenant Colonel Algernon S. Taylor. This native of Alexandria was commissioned in the Provisional Army of Virginia and was the nephew of former president Zachary Taylor. On May 3, the battalion took an all-night train ride from the Orange and Alexandria (O&A) Railroad station to the Culpeper Court House sixty miles away. When the men discovered an error by a telegraph operator, who wrote "Battalion" instead of "Battery," they returned on the morning train minus the Alexandria Artillery.

Receiving travel orders on May 5, the battalion left by train at 11:00 p.m. This time, it reached Springfield Station, ten miles away, before it found the orders were a mistake. By noon on the seventh, the men were back in Alexandria. This time, authorities questioned Colonel Taylor about his premature evacuation of the city. He reported that the withdrawal was due to the inefficient condition of a large part of his battalion and the vulnerability of his exposed and indefensible position. Taylor wrote that the two Irish companies, totaling about 240 privates, were armed with altered flintlocks without cartridges or caps. The Mount Vernon Guard had new muskets, but 52 of the 86 privates were without accouterments, 15 were without arms and very few had much ammunition. The 53 Warren Rifles had Minié rifles with nine rounds each, while the 85 rank and file of the Old Dominion Rifles had Minié rifles with an average of five rounds and four caps each. Although Taylor's report did not include the Alexandria Rifles, another made on about the same date reported that the 69 men had fifty muskets and no ammunition. The 40 privates of Captain Mottrom Ball's cavalry company had carbines and sabers but a limited amount of ammunition. The Fairfax Cavalry numbered 30, with only twenty-two mounts and only a few Colt revolvers.

The authorities in Richmond and Potomac Department headquarters at Culpeper Court House were evidently not satisfied with Taylor's report. He lost his command on May 10. His replacement was Colonel George Hunter Terrett, who had resigned from the U.S. Marine Corps on April 22 and had been commissioned as a colonel by May 7. Major Corse had served as assistant under Taylor and continued in that capacity under the new commander.

The arrival of the gunboat USS *Pawnee* near Alexandria on May 10 caused quite a bit of excitement. Concern arose over the increased possibility of an enemy advance from Washington City. Guards were placed at the foot of Cameron Street to keep an eye on the blockading steamer. Those not on guard duty were regularly at drill by squad, by company and by battalion—occasionally under the command of Colonel Terrett.

On May 18, another Irish company, the O'Connell Guard, was organized under Captain Stephen W. Prestman and composed largely of railroad workers. The *Alexandria Gazette* of May 23 carried an appeal for ladies to help make uniforms for the new company.

DEATH OF COL. ELLSWORTH.

A tinted lithograph of the confrontation between Colonel Elmer E. Ellsworth and James W. Jackson in the Marshall House. The North and South had immediate martyrs.

It was also on May 23, 1861, that the polls opened in Alexandria for the purpose of voting on ratification of the ordinance of secession. Only 106 voted in opposition, while 983 ratified the ordinance. About 400 registered voters did not go to the polls—they had probably already left Alexandria for Richmond. By 2:00 a.m. on the twenty-fourth, Union troops had crossed the Potomac River bridges into Virginia. Steamers carrying the Eleventh New York Fire Zouaves under Colonel Ellsworth arrived at the foot of King Street. As the Zouaves landed, Private William Todd Morrill of the Alexandria Riflemen fired the first rifle shot of the war against an enemy foe on Virginia soil. Morrill and his fellow pickets began falling back toward the city. At about 3:00 a.m., Captain Simpson rushed to his Warren Rifles. "Wake up, boys!" he cried. "They are coming! By George, they are across the bridge!"

Lieutenant Reigart B. Lowry, U.S. Navy, left the *Pawnee* at about 4:30 a.m. to meet with Colonel Terrett and demand the surrender of Alexandria. The surrender was refused, and Terrett announced that he would evacuate the city. He ordered the battalion to assemble at Lyceum Hall and await further orders. Learning of the enemy approach by Washington Street, the battalion was ordered to depart by way of Duke Street at about 6:50 a.m. The Old Dominion Rifles were almost captured when they were late getting the order. Lieutenant Herbert managed to get his riflemen up to the retreating column as it moved westward on Duke Street and avoided their capture. As they evacuated the city, they were told that James Jackson had killed Colonel Ellsworth and was, himself, killed instantly by Private Francis Brownell while attempting to retrieve the Confederate flag Ellsworth had removed from the roof of the Marshall House.

The retreat was covered by two cavalry units: Captain Edward Powell's Fairfax Cavalry and Captain Mottrom Ball's Chesterfield Troop. Terrett reported that his Virginians, "five hundred in number, retreated in good order." The Union troops were hard on the tail of Terrett's force, whose rear guard was "in sight of and within two hundred yards of the advance guard of the enemy." Given the apparent aggressiveness of the pursuit, one wonders how sincere of a choice Terrett was given between surrender and evacuation.

Ball accompanied Terrett and his men as far as a little west of the railroad depot on the O&A. The volunteers continued for a half mile beyond the depot, where they boarded cars for Manassas. Terrett asked the cavalry to follow in his rear, but for whatever reason, Ball's thirty-five men took too long and were captured by Federals, the First Michigan Infantry under

A lithograph of the surrender of Captain Mottrom Ball and his troopers near the Alexandria Slave Pen. They became the first POWs outside Charleston, South Carolina.

Colonel Orlando B. Wilcox. Captain Ball and his troopers were taken to the Washington Navy Yard, the first POWs of the war in Northern Virginia. About a month later, they were released, after taking the oath of allegiance to the United States. They immediately headed South and rejoined the Confederate forces.

Just west of the O&A depot, Terrett's command stopped several trains returning from Springfield Station. The entire command boarded trains and traveled twenty-seven miles to Manassas Junction. Immediately afterward, Confederate forces destroyed twenty-two miles of track and all the bridges from Cameron Run to Fairfax Station.

As mentioned, the first Union troops crossed the Potomac River into Alexandria County during the early morning hours of May 24, 1861. An officer reported that it was a beautiful moonlit night, and the moonbeams glittered brightly on the flashing muskets as the regiment silently advanced across the Long Bridge.

THE UNION INVADERS/LIBERATORS

Eight Union regiments under the command of Colonel J.F.K. Mansfield crossed the river and took up positions in Virginia early on May 24. The first unit to cross was one under Major W.H. Wood, which moved via the

Aqueduct Bridge (near the present Key Bridge) from Georgetown and then out the Georgetown Wagon Road (present Wilson Boulevard) and camped near present-day Clarendon.

The second unit was the Seventh New York Infantry under Major Samuel P. Heintzelman, which marched over the Long Bridge (the present Fourteenth Street Bridge) and reached the Virginia side at about 4:00 a.m. The third, under Colonel Ellsworth, proceeded by water to the city of Alexandria.

The only opposition encountered by Union troops was from some pickets at the southern end of the Long Bridge and in Alexandria Harbor. There were no casualties. Confederate volunteer units withdrew in good order.

Arlington House, the recently vacated home of Robert E. Lee and his family, was occupied almost immediately. General Charles W. Sandford of the Eighth New York State Militia established his headquarters there.

By the time the first Union troops arrived in Alexandria County, many officials known to be Confederate sympathizers had left. This included military and law enforcement officers, as well as the clerk of courts. People remaining after the troops came were Union sympathizers or "quiet" Confederates.

The Union regiments established camps, performed picket duty and later built part of the defenses of Washington City on high ground near the Potomac River and up to about five miles away from the river. Companies from both the First Michigan Infantry and the Eleventh New York Infantry performed picket duty and camped at Arlington Mills, about five miles from the Long Bridge.

On the night of June 1, 1861, Company E of the First Michigan Infantry was camped in the Arlington Mill while on picket duty, and Company G of the Eleventh New York Infantry, having come to relieve the First, was in a nearby house. At about 11:00 p.m., a squad of Virginia militiamen, which contemporary newspaper accounts stated was only nine in number, approached the Union sentinels and camps and fired a volley. At least one newspaper account stated that the Michigan men in the mill and the nearby Zouaves fired on one another, as well as at the Virginians, in the confusion. In any event, the Virginians were quickly driven off. The Union forces suffered one killed—twenty-one-year-old Henry S. Cornell of Company G, a member of Engine Co. 13—and one injured. The Confederates suffered one wounded.

Following the skirmish at Arlington Mills and the "battle" at Fairfax Court House on the same day, the Union Army did not attempt to move farther into Northern Virginia until June 17, 1861, when a Union reconnaissance

A lithograph of U.S. troops preparing to cross the Long Bridge over the Potomac to take over Arlington. It was reported that "the moonlight glinted off the bayonets." *Courtesy of Douglas Bostick.*

in force led to the Battle of Vienna. Many of these early "battles" would not even rate as skirmishes after First Manassas/Bull Run.

The Eleventh New York Infantry fought at First Manassas, where it suffered many casualties and hundreds taken prisoner, as well as some desertions. The regiment was never successfully reorganized and eventually was mustered out of service. Many of its men reenlisted in other New York regiments.

Anne Frobel recorded in her diary:

> *A long time after—a year or perhaps two, I met with some Confederate scouts, Captain Kinchelow was one of them, and he told me, how those vile brutal Zouaves had behaved at our house, and at other places, how they had mal-treated and tyrannized over the citizens generally, and they had determined with one accord if it was ever in their power to make an end of them. Their conspicuous dress made them a ready mark, and he did not believe when the battle [First Manassas] was over there was one left to tell the tale.*

Prior to 1870, the city of Alexandria was part of Alexandria County. The "country" part of the county beyond the city's boundaries (essentially consisting of the area that is now Arlington County) was a rural community inhabited primarily by people dependent on farming for their livelihood. A number of landowners were residents of Washington City or the city of Alexandria and visited their country landholdings from time to time. Other than farming, there were only two occupations that might be called industry. A brickyard was located near the southern end of the Long Bridge, and milling operations were located primarily along Four Mile Run, including the Arlington Mill near the crossing of Columbia Turnpike.

Construction of the earliest fortifications in Arlington required about seven weeks—to mid-July 1861. Forts were thrown up right and left, trenches cut through pastures and gardens, forests cut down and troop encampments all about. Possession of property in Arlington was taken with little or no reference to the rights of owners or occupants of the premises, according to Union major general J.G. Barnard writing at a later date.

The first goal was to build fortifications to protect the bridges across the Potomac. Fort Corcoran overlooked the Aqueduct Bridge (Key Bridge).

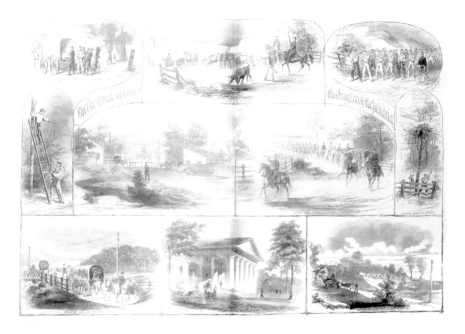

Another *Harper's Weekly* lithograph portraying locales and events in and around Alexandria, Virginia.

A lithograph from *Harper's Weekly* portraying the Union army early in the war. Note the "General Beauregard" target practice.

To protect it, Fort Bennett (above Rosslyn) and Fort Haggerty (opposite Roosevelt Island) were built.

Fort Runyon was located astride the important junction of the Washington, Alexandria and Columbia Turnpikes, a half mile south of the Long Bridge. The largest fort in the defenses of Washington, it covered twelve acres and had a perimeter of 1,484 yards. Construction began on May 24, 1861, and was completed in seven weeks. Fort Albany was built on the high ground to protect the rear of Fort Runyon (under present-day I-395, near Overlook Park at South Nash Street and South Arlington Ridge Road).

Congress and the general public believed that the war would be short. Socialites and other curious civilians gathered at First Manassas on July 21, 1861. Union forces were defeated and retreated toward Arlington, Alexandria and Washington City.

After First Manassas, both the North and the South realized that the war was not going to be short. The Federal capital was even more vulnerable to invasion. The military recognized not only the need to greatly improve defenses for Washington but also to retrain and better equip the Union army.

Arlington Heights was strengthened by connecting all forts from Fort Corcoran to Fort Albany (from Key Bridge to the Fourteenth Street Bridge).

Accordingly, a number of "lunettes" were built: Forts Craig, Tillinghast, Cass and Woodbury. Next, Fort DeKalb (later called Fort Strong) was built near today's Lee Highway and Spout Run Parkway. In 1863, new works were added: Forts Whipple (now Fort Myer), Berry and C.F. Smith.

A total of twenty-two out of forty-eight defensive works protecting Washington City constructed during the entire war were located in the country part of Alexandria County.

After First Manassas, Munson's Hill (located between Seven Corners and Bailey's Cross Roads) became the site of a Confederate signal station and of the famous Confederate "Quaker guns"—logs painted to look like artillery pieces.

A Union Private's Impressions of Alexandria

The following is taken from a letter by Private John Vautier, a soldier in the Eighty-eighth Pennsylvania Volunteer Infantry, shortly after their arrival in October to provide provost duty there:

Clear and cold weather. Rearranged our camp, and in the afternoon we all went to church where Washington went. It is an Episcopalian Church. Alexandria is a very ordinary looking place of about 8,000 or 9,000 inhabitants. A great many of the people have left and gone to hunt the "Confederacy" up. I guess they will get enough of the "Confederacy" before they are through. Scarcely a young man can be seen. The Rebs raised a Battery here and called it Keplers because Kepler commanded it. Here too is the place where the "high bred Southern Ladies" turn their noses up at poor Yankee Mudsills like us, and turn another street to avoid us. The only place of interest is the house where poor Ellsworth was killed. The staircase is almost all torn away by eager relic hunters, but as for me I was content with standing on the spot where he breathed his last, and where the blood of Jackson stained the floor. I contented myself with contemplating on the great spirit who died here. And right here in this doorway is where the infamous Jackson died too. Retribution speedily overtook him. And these are the steps where they carried Ellsworth down, and this is the doorway—Yes all these are sacred places. Sacred to the memory of every American.

African Americans in Alexandria

For the first year of the Civil War, the Lincoln administration held out hope of reuniting the Union without total war. This and fears of alienating the slaveholding border states, which included Maryland, Delaware, Missouri and Kentucky, made the U.S. government continue to respect Federal and state laws that kept most African Americans in slavery. In fact, many army field commanders returned runaway slaves to their owners under the Fugitive Slave Law still in force. But the soldiers and many politicians became increasingly angry and dissatisfied with the situation as the flood of fugitives increased, and the Confederate armies employed the labor of the remaining slaves.

The following article, from the *Washington National Republican* of January 20, 1862, was taken from a letter addressed to Massachusetts antislavery senator Henry Wilson. It expresses outrage at the poor conditions and inhumanity of treatment of slaves in the Alexandria Jail, even under Federal occupation. It points out that the actions of the Union authorities at that date were actually propping up slavery. It also makes clear that the jail functioned much as a low-class dog pound would today—runaway slaves were captured and placed in a cell until their owners appeared, or for a fee, owners could simply drop off slaves for safekeeping while out of town, etc. The passage below does mention a few names: slaves Cynthia Brent and Benhood (or Ben Hood) and owners Mr. Close, Mr. Swan and Mrs. Kitson.

In the Senate, on January 14, 1862, Mr. Wilson read the following portions of a letter addressed to him by Dr. Samuel G. Howe (Dr. Howe was married to Julia Ward Howe, author of the "Battle Hymn of the Republic"):

> *I thank you for your work on behalf of the poor fugitive slaves confined in the jail here* [Alexandria]…
>
> *Last June* [1861] *I tried in vain to do something for these victims of our impolicy. I pleaded with one member of the Cabinet to do something for them; and described the condition of thirty-five men, women, and children then held in bonds by the United States marshal for the benefit of their owners.*
>
> *But you have appealed to the great heart of the people, and they will cheer you on by a shout of indignation at the atrocities perpetrated under the very walls of the Capitol.*

The same atrocities are practiced under the same authority in the jail at Alexandria, which I lately inspected. The building is a wretched one, totally unfit for a public prison. It seems to have been built in the days when accused persons were considered as public enemies, and to be caged like wild beasts. The cells are narrow, dark, and damp, and the rings and staples fixed in some of the walls tell their own story. The internal arrangements are very bad; and the general condition of the house is filthy and noisome to the last degree. Such a jail would be presented by the grand jury in any Northern city as an intolerable nuisance. The system of administration is disgraceful to any State claiming to be Christian and civilized. The jail is rented out to an individual for $400 a year, who hires a turnkey and other assistants, and boards the prisoners for thirty-five cents a day.

In the case of negroes who are arrested for being without free papers or passes, the board is paid by the master when he comes for them. If no claimant appears, and the poor fellow cannot prove that he is free, he is kept until the fees amount to a sum, when he may be sold to satisfy the claims of injustice.

Among the prisoners are nineteen whose only offence is that of fleeing from those who claimed to be their masters. Some of them have been confined several months; but, in spite of all the horrors of the place, they do not want to be sent back to their masters, because they fear "being sold down South." I saw fifteen of these unfortunate creatures, and spent time enough to ascertain the exact truth respecting their history and condition. I examined what are called "the books," and such wretchedly written memoranda respecting their commitment as exist.

I had a peremptory order from the commandant upon the jailer to give me all information, and he did so, evidently being in great fear of the authorities. I conversed with the prisoners in his presence, and then alone; so that I got pretty good evidence...

Let me note some of these cases to show how loosely injustice is administered in the sacred soil of Virginia by the United States authorities. You may infer what must have been the former state of things.

The records show that, on the 9th of August, 1861, Cynthia Brent was taken up by somebody, and put in the jail as a supposed runaway slave. On the 29th of August, a Mr. Close, who had owned the girl's father, obtained an order for the chattel, and took her away. She escaped from him, but fell into the hands of her master, Mr. Swan, who brought her, on the 10th of September, and imprisoned her on his own authority, and she is still in prison.

Alexandria County Is Liberated/Invaded

On the 16th of August, 1861, came one Mrs. Kitson—she ought not to have any Christian name—and claiming four fugitives—two women, one "boy," and one child—as her slaves; and, as she paid their board, she took them off, probably to sell them to other "beasts of burden."

June 12, 1861, was brought in Benhood, a fugitive. He was kept nearly five months, and probably began to think he was safe; but, on the 6th of November, one Fleming, claiming to be agent of his master—now himself a fugitive—came with an order from General Montgomery, and carried poor Benhood off to a known fate in unknown parts.

The persons claiming to own these human beings are, for the most part, rebels, and have fled; the United States acts as jailor, and takes care of their chattels during their absence.

On June 8, Tennessee, the final Confederate state, seceded:

DECLARATION OF INDEPENDENCE AND ORDINANCE dissolving the federal relations between the State of Tennessee and the United States of America.

We, the people of the State of Tennessee, waiving any expression of opinion as to the abstract doctrine of secession, but asserting the right, as a free and independent people, to alter, reform, or abolish our form of government in such manner as we think proper, do ordain and declare that all the laws and ordinances by which the State of Tennessee became a member of the Federal Union of the United States of America are hereby abrogated and annulled, and that all the rights, functions, and powers which by any of said laws and ordinances were conveyed to the Government of the United States, and to absolve ourselves from all the obligations, restraints, and duties incurred thereto; and do hereby henceforth become a free, sovereign, and independent State...

Sent to referendum 6 May 1861 by the legislature, and approved by the voters by a vote of 104,471 to 47,183 on 8 June 1861.

4

Fairfax County

Mount Vernon—Neutral Haven in a Divided Nation

Today, Mount Vernon is the most visited historical mansion in all of Virginia. Things were extremely different in the middle of the nineteenth century. After the deaths of George Washington in 1799 and his widow, Martha, in 1802, Mount Vernon remained in the family for three generations. By the 1850s, the home was beginning to crumble. John Augustine Washington Jr., a great-great-nephew of George Washington, was left without enough money to take care of the home and property. To his credit, John Washington would not sell to commercial developers and insisted that the new owner preserve Mount Vernon as a historic site. He offered to sell the estate to either the Federal government or the Commonwealth of Virginia, but both declined, saying it would not be proper to spend taxpayers' money to acquire private property. When the men of America failed to act, it was left to the ladies to take responsibility.

In 1853, the night boat had gone down the Potomac River from Alexandria, carrying its usual load of travelers. About ten miles below the city, the ship's bell began to toll dolefully. The boat went slowly past the Mount Vernon mansion. Ghostly, gaunt and gray, it stood, an ominous sight, enfolded in river mist and lighted by the moon. Among the passengers was Mrs. Louise Dalton Bird Cunningham of South Carolina, who had grown up in Alexandria and visited Mount Vernon years earlier when she was a child. Then it had been a stately white mansion, its lawn cut and its shrubbery trimmed. She saw that unless something was done quickly, the famous old house would fall into ruins, overrun by brambles and briars. She

Mount Vernon as it appears today—the most visited tourist destination in Northern Virginia. *Courtesy of the Library of Congress.*

wondered if anyone could save the place from irreparable harm. Suddenly, she thought it was the *women* of America who should repair and preserve Mount Vernon—mansion, grounds and tomb.

She wrote to her invalid daughter, Ann Pamela Cunningham, "If the men of America have seen fit to allow the home of its most respected hero to go to ruin, why can't the women of America band together to save it?" As she finished reading her mother's letter, Ann exclaimed, "I will do it!" All of her strength and energy that she had put into living before a fall from her horse had made her an invalid, she put into planning a way to buy and maintain Mount Vernon. She wrote a letter to the editor of the *Charleston Mercury*, appealing to American women to come to the rescue of Mount Vernon. She invited influential women from each state (there were thirty-one at that time) to serve as the original vice regents of the Mount Vernon Ladies' Association (MLVA), which was the first national women's organization in America. She became its first regent. Brilliant and talented women stepped forward from each state to become the first vice regents. John A. Washington agreed to sell the mansion and two hundred surrounding acres for $200,000.

Miss Cunningham and the association launched a nationwide fundraising effort. The initial intent was for the association to raise the money, which would be deposited in Richmond to allow Virginia to purchase the property and then assign care of the estate to the association. However, that arrangement proved unworkable. When, in March 1858, Virginia's House of Delegates defeated a bill for the purchase of Mount Vernon, John Washington agreed to sell directly to the association, and the contract was signed in Richmond on April 6, 1858. The gold pen used by Miss Cunningham remains in the possession of the MVLA. The agreement was to sell the mansion, outbuildings and two hundred surrounding acres to the association for $200,000, with an immediate down payment of $18,000 and the balance to be paid in four installments, payable on February 22 (Washington's birthday) each of the next four years. The Massachusetts orator Edward Everett (most famous today for his two-hour speech before President Lincoln's two-minute "Gettysburg Address" in November 1863) went on a speaking tour to raise money. The association raised the capital in about eighteen months, announcing that it had met its goal in mid-December 1859. The MVLA, in a symbolic gesture, took formal possession on Washington's birthday, when John Washington and his family moved out of the mansion on February 22, 1860. To demonstrate the nationwide scope of the organization on the eve of war between North and South, the association appended its name to the Mount Vernon Ladies' Association of the Union.

In June 1859, Sarah Tracy of Troy, New York, was interviewed for the job of secretary of the MVLA. A few months after this, the *Mount Vernon Record* (official newsletter of the association) announced:

> *We are happy to see that the Regent is fulfilling her promise of carrying on the work of repairs at Mount Vernon as rapidly as possible. We noticed that workmen placed there by Mr. Washington, are under the supervision of Mr. Upton H. Herbert* [brother of Arthur Herbert], *who is, by ancestry, closely allied with the history of Mount Vernon. His great-grandmother was a daughter of William Fairfax, and her sister married Lawrence Washington. This connection makes the appointment appropriate, as he feels a personal pride in maintaining the Mansion.*

Sarah Tracy of Troy, New York, was secretary of the Mount Vernon Ladies'
Association during the Civil War and was the main driving force in preserving Mount
Vernon as neutral territory.

Except for furniture Mr. Herbert brought from his own home and a few
pieces left by John Washington, the house was empty. The work of repairing,
furnishing and then beautifying Mount Vernon lay ahead of the ladies, and
Miss Cunningham begged Herbert not to abandon his post in the event of war.

In the late fall of 1860, Miss Cunningham was called home to South Carolina. While she was gone, Miss Tracy continued shopping for furniture, curtains and carpets to make the mansion a comfortable headquarters for her when she returned. She wrote, "The house looks very much better than I anticipated, though some rooms are shabby enough, still we can make it very comfortable. I shall have to make some purchases in Alexandria. There are hardly any kitchen utensils at all, and an absolute necessity is window shades for the library, or curtains."

In March 1861, Miss Tracy was still expecting Miss Cunningham to return from South Carolina and go with her to Mt. Vernon. Her letters, written to the regent during the war years, are a study in quiet charm and unflinching character. She eventually wrote, "I have found the troubles of today as to annihilate those of yesterday, and those of tomorrow too far off to command attention." Some of the upkeep was defrayed by the twenty-five cents charged to visitors to see the mansion and tomb.

April 12, 1861, saw the firing upon Fort Sumter and the start of the war. On April 13, Sarah wrote, "I am writing without the least idea that you will receive my letter, for I suppose the mails will be stopped. This war news has completely unnerved me. May God forgive the ring leaders and provokers of such evil, both sides! Heaven only can see the end. It cuts into my heart whichever way I look."

Two days later, a story appeared in the *New York Herald* that caused great excitement in Alexandria and Washington City. It told that the body of George Washington had been removed from his tomb and taken away to the mountains of Virginia.

Upon reading the article, Sarah wrote at once to the *National Intelligencer*, a leading Washington City newspaper:

We are requested by the ladies of the Mount Vernon Association to state that the assertion which appeared in the **New York Herald** *of the 15th instant to the effect that Col. J.A. Washington had caused the removal of the remains of General Washington from Mount Vernon is utterly false and without foundation. Never, since first laid in this his chosen resting place, have the remains of our Great Father reposed more quietly and peacefully than now, when the entire outer world is distracted by warlike thoughts and deeds. And the public, the owners of this noble possession, need fear no molestation of this one national spot belonging alike to North and South. Over it there can be no dispute! No individual or individuals has the right, and surely none can have the inclination, to disturb this sacred trust. The*

Fairfax County: Mount Vernon

Ladies have taken every necessary precaution for the protection of the place, and their earnest desire is that the public should feel confidence in their faithfulness to their trust, and believe that Mount Vernon is safe under the guardianship of the Ladies of the Mount Vernon Association of the Union.

The last week in April, Sarah went to Alexandria and found it wild with excitement. She wrote to Miss Cunningham, telling her of the long lines of refugees pouring in from Washington City and of her difficulty in finding a woman who would accompany her to Mount Vernon as a chaperone, to be with her until her friend, Mary McMakin, should arrive from Philadelphia. She felt sure they would be perfectly safe at Mount Vernon in the midst of the rapidly approaching war and added, "If Mr. Herbert is obliged to fight, and he may be, we will take care of Mount Vernon! Mr. Herbert has formed a Home Guard in the neighborhood."

Miss Cunningham wrote that if Washington should become the seat of a terrible conflict, it might be well for Herbert to stop the Mount Vernon boat from running in order to safeguard the mansion. Before he could take steps to stop the boat from running, however, the move was made unnecessary. The U.S. government seized the *Thomas Collyer* and turned it into a troop transport.

On May 2, Sarah wrote:

Mr. Herbert told the Captain of the Company of soldiers stationed near here [Confederates] *your wishes with regard to their not coming here in uniform or armed. They have behaved very well about it. Many of them come from a very long distance and have never been here, and have no clothes but their uniforms. They borrow shawls and cover up their buttons and leave their arms outside the enclosures, and never come but two or three at a time. That is as much as can be asked of them. Mr. Herbert has resisted every tempting offer to join the* [Southern] *Army. He has had several. Both his brothers, and every friend he has, have done so, and they wonder much that he has refused the command of every company offered. He says very little about it, but has, I know, made a sacrifice for Mount Vernon. Alas, how sad all this makes us and what a change has come over the spirit of our dream.*

When rumors spread through Virginia that Federal troops might be placed at Mount Vernon, Sarah went to Washington, where she attempted to meet with General Winfield Scott. At the door of the general's office, she found an

Ann Pamela Cunningham, the savior of the Mount Vernon estate. She established the Mount Vernon Ladies' Association, the first such organization in the United States. During the Civil War, the estate was declared "neutral territory." *Courtesy of the Library of Congress.*

officer she knew. Major Edward D. Townsend proclaimed it was impossible to see the general. But unable to withstand her pleading, the major went to the general's desk and told him of the neutral position that the Mount Vernon Ladies were attempting to maintain at the mansion.

Sarah heard the general exclaim, "God bless the Ladies!" When the major came out, he told her, "The general wishes me to assure you that no troops shall be placed at Mount Vernon under any plea whatsoever and asks if you can be equally sure of Virginia?"

For the entire state of Virginia, she unhesitatingly answered, "Yes!"

Sarah wrote to Miss Cunningham on May 11:

I wish you were here. Everything is so beautiful and peaceful one cannot realize that at so short a distance from us men's passions are driving them to all that is wicked and horrible. Mother earth promises bountiful supplies from her store house to keep us from want, even if foreign luxuries are cut off. The strawberry vines and the fruit trees are laden. But sugar and coffee we must go without.

Upton Herbert wrote to Miss Cunningham on May 16:

I had the honor of receiving your letter of the 12th inst. All of your suggestions, in regard to the preservation and protection of Mount Vernon, shall be attended to. Miss Tracy will have informed you, ere this, of her interview with the powers that be in Washington. I think I can influence the soldiers of the Confederate Army, by stating to them your wishes, in regard to their visiting at Mount Vernon: but as it is your wish, I will see Colonel Terrett, who commands the troops in this vicinity.

*The bedroom of General Washington has been replastered and painted.
The leaks in the roof have been stopped; so that it will not be necessary, at
this time, to reroof.*

Mr. Riggs [George Washington Riggs, prominent Washington
banker and treasurer of the MVLA] *has informed me that I must
discharge the workers, as there is no money now to defray the expense of
keeping them. Mr. Washington's farm houses are too far away to be injured
by guns from the fort.*

WAR COMES TO VIRGINIA AND MOUNT VERNON

A week after this letter, the Northern army, under cover of darkness, crossed
the Potomac and seized the city of Alexandria. Most of the Southern
soldiers in the city were warned in time to escape and reassemble near
Manassas Junction. Arlington, the home of Robert and Mary Ann Lee, was
also captured by Northern troops. Mary Lee was the daughter of George
Washington Parke Custis, grandson of Martha and adopted son of George
Washington. The house was full of furniture, china and ornaments belonging
to Martha and George. When Mary heard that Northern soldiers would be
"liberating" Arlington, she ordered a farm wagon to the house. She took as
much of the furniture as she could and headed into the Virginia countryside.

After Union troops took Alexandria, mail service for the Mount Vernon
neighborhood was discontinued. The small U.S. Post Office at Accotink was
too far inside Confederate lines to have any contact with Alexandria and
Washington City and was too far north to be given Southern postal service.
Letters had to be carried by special messenger either to Alexandria to the
north or below Occoquan to the south.

Sarah wrote to Miss Cunningham on June 6, "We are hoping for a Post
Office at Occoquan, eight miles from here…Roof leaking badly again. We
heard all the firing at the time of the attack on Aquia Creek [May 29, in
Stafford County]. It is fortunate that I am here, for from no other place, I
know, could I communicate both ways." She wrote again on June 8, "There
is no Southern communication with Alexandria, and our letters are suddenly
stopped. I may be able to send you a letter occasionally. You had better write
me by way of Kentucky."

Sarah made a trip to the War Department in Washington to ask permission
to send letters from Mount Vernon to Miss Cunningham. She was told to

make sure her letters did not contain any military information. On June 17, she wrote:

> *I am known as a Northerner and Mr. Herbert as a Virginian. Mr. Herbert was advised not to go to Alexandria again. He had decided not to before, for he would not risk being examined and forced to take the oath. I went to town and got passes and saw Mr. Burke* [a founder of Burke and Herbert Bank]. *Washington and Alexandria are military cities. The entire outskirts are one great camp ground. It is strange how quiet it is within these grounds; though we hear firing outside occasionally.*

July commenced quietly, but the second week of July found the neighborhood wild with excitement. The Confederates had proclaimed July 15 as Muster Day, and many men who did not wish to be drafted unwillingly into the Southern army were attempting to reach the outposts of the Northern troops. The religious principles of the Quakers in the Mount Vernon neighborhood were being respected by the Confederates, but there was scarcely a Friends' household that did not have one young man in a gray uniform while a few miles away another son was wearing a blue one. The Quakers, many originally from New Jersey, were to suffer not only the hardships of war but also the tragedy of divided loyalty.

On July 15, Sarah wrote to Mrs. Comegys, vice regent for Delaware:

> *I shall now remain here as long as it may seem best for the sake of Mount Vernon. I am glad I have remained, though, for my own sake, I have wished a thousand times that I was in China! The only correspondence from Mount Vernon to the South are letters to Miss Cunningham, and a very neutral place it would be, if the Regent cannot be permitted to hear what is going on here!*

On July 22, Sarah wrote:

> *Before this letter reaches you, you will have heard the news of the terrible fight at Bull Run. I have considerable strength of mind, but it was tried to the utmost yesterday. The wind was south on Thursday and we did not hear much of the firing in the afternoon, when for two hours it was very distinct. But yesterday we will none of us forget. At six o'clock in the morning, I was aroused by cannon, and from then until one o'clock there was not three minutes, no hardly one minute between firings. Then, for half an hour it ceased; recommencing*

and continuing with equal rapidity 'til six o'clock, when there was an hour's cessation. Then it commenced again and continuing until dark.

After the battle, life at Mount Vernon slowly returned to relative normalcy, until it was again shattered by General Order No. 13 from General Scott on July 31:

It has been the prayer of every patriot that the tramp and din of Civil War might at least spare the precincts within which repose the remains of the Father of this Country, but this pious hope is disappointed. Mount Vernon, so recently consecrated to the Immortal Washington by the Ladies of America, has been overrun by bands of rebels, who, having trampled under foot the Constitution of the United States, the ark of our freedom and prosperity, are prepared to tramp on the ashes of him to whom we are all mainly indebted for these mighty blessings. Should the operations of our war take the United States troops in that direction, the General Officer does not doubt that every man will approach with due reverence, and leave undisturbed, not only the Tomb, but also the house, groves and walks which were so loved by the best and greatest of men.

Immediately, Sarah sent out a response to the newspapers:

The officers of the Mount Vernon Association are pained to see, in today's issue, an order from Lieutenant-General Scott containing a statement which they fear will lead to much trouble and misunderstanding. General Scott has been misinformed as to the facts. The statement referred to is that Mount Vernon has been "overrun by bands of rebels." Since the occupation of Alexandria by Federal troops, not a single soldier from the Southern Army has visited Mount Vernon. It is but justice to say that the intruders who refused to accede to the regulations of the Association, heretofore willingly followed by the soldiers from both sides, were a company of New York Volunteers, headed by their Colonel and other officers. The Regent is earnest and decided in her request and direction to those she has made responsible for the preservation of order and neutrality at Mount Vernon and in the discharge of this sacred duty they have been kindly aided by those at Headquarters of the Army. It is, therefore, to them a source of great regret to be obliged to correct such a mistake; as it is much easier to excite than to allay unkind feelings.

Sarah got to Washington City and received another pass and order from General Scott.

SARAH AND THE BONDS

When the Federal troops took Alexandria, the money and bonds that had been paid by the Mount Vernon Ladies' Association to John Washington were in a safe in the Burke & Herbert Bank. One of the bank's founders was Arthur Herbert, a brother of Upton Herbert. In September, news was received that Colonel John A. Washington had been killed near Cheat Mountain in Virginia. He had been on the staff of General Robert E. Lee. An order was sent out from U.S. Army headquarters that John Washington's money was to be confiscated. One morning, a Northern officer, with a few men, entered the bank and demanded the money. The man in charge of the bank told the searching party that he knew nothing about the safe, that John W. Burke was out of the bank at the moment and that Mr. Herbert was with the Confederate army. The officer and his men left the bank, planning to return when they could talk to Mr. Burke.

As soon as they had left, Mr. Burke returned and was told of their visit. He opened the safe, took out the money and bonds, left the bank and went to his own home. He went to his room, placed the package containing the money and bonds in a large mahogany wardrobe and pulled clothing down to cover the package. He then hurried back to the bank.

Just after he entered the bank, he heard the soldiers returning. It took him some time to convince the searchers that the money was neither in the safe nor in the bank. They realized that in some way they had been tricked, and upon leaving the bank, they went directly to Burke's house. The officer in charge insisted on speaking to Mrs. Burke, who had just returned from her drive and knew nothing of the package hidden on the floor of the wardrobe. Annoyed by the time he had already spent on his futile

John W. Burke with his son Julian shortly before the Civil War. One of the founders of Burke & Herbert Bank, he stayed in Alexandria to keep the bank solvent while Arthur Herbert joined the Confederate army.

mission, the officer ordered a search of the house. Basement to attic was ransacked, with bureau drawers overturned and private papers scattered. Only the lady's wardrobe escaped careful scrutiny. Unable to find what he had been sent for, the officer and his men withdrew, promising to return.

As soon as word reached the bank that Union soldiers had carried out an unsuccessful search of his house, Burke quietly left the bank. The usually peaceful streets were overcrowded with hurrying soldiers and civilians from the North. He found a carpenter he could trust and took him to his house, where the carpenter lifted a hallway floorboard and hid the package.

The next day, another officer and soldiers came to search the house. "It does not seem right to me," said Mrs. Burke, "that the great-granddaughter of one of the presidents of the United States should be obliged to accept such indignities at the hands of her countrymen." Martha Burke, who had been born at Monticello, was the great-granddaughter of Thomas Jefferson.

"No it does not seem right," agreed the young officer. He proved as quiet and courteous as the previous day's officer had been noisy and rude. Nevertheless, the searchers were thorough, even searching the wardrobe. Yet as they walked along the hallway, the package remained carefully hidden.

The following day, Sarah drove out the long road from Mount Vernon. No one could accompany her. Mr. Herbert had no pass through the Federal lines. She drove through scattered groups of soldiers and camps. Some days, she would bring a load of cabbages to sell at the city market in order to raise money for the repairs at Mount Vernon. On this day, she had a basket of fresh eggs.

When she reached Alexandria, she called at the home of her friends Mr. and Mrs. Burke. After she had been seated for a few moments, John Burke asked, "Would you be willing to do a great service for the Washington family?"

"I will do anything for them that is within my power," she replied without hesitation.

In a low tone, Burke told her what he would have her do and then left the room to get the package. Sarah sat for a few moments deep in thought and then removed the eggs from her basket. Mrs. Burke silently nodded her approval. When Mr. Burke returned, Sarah motioned him to place the package in the bottom of the basket. Carefully replacing the eggs, she placed the basket on her arm and said goodbye.

Seated in her little wagon with the basket of eggs beside her, she looked as lovely and helpless as any Victorian lady of that era. She rode down the streets of Alexandria, past thousands of Union troops and, armed with her Federal pass, crossed over the bridge and entered Washington City. She drove directly to Mr. Riggs's office in his bank, rented a safety deposit box, placed the package with money and bonds inside and locked the box. Then, with a brief explanation and farewell to Mr. Riggs, she drove back across the Potomac and gave the key to Burke. To avoid suspicion, she had left the eggs on Riggs's desk, and he had tucked the egg money into her purse.

She drove slowly back along the old road to Mount Vernon. In Alexandria, the search continued for the missing money and bonds. She wrote a letter to Mrs. Comegys but did not say a word about her adventure:

> *I must visit Washington again to procure passes. General McClellan has taken command, and there are new regulations. All passes must come from his office or General Scott's. None of the servants can go to Alexandria, and we have had mail but once in ten days! I must get proper passes or go myself three times a week to Alexandria—or go without mail. This I cannot think of, for I must keep watch lest anything against Mount Vernon appears. For two miles this side of Alexandria, until I reach Mr. Riggs', it is nothing but soldiers in the street and on the boat. Then all the camps to pass through! For the rest of my life I shall have a dislike for a gun, or a drum, or a military uniform! Martial music that I used to love above all others is nothing but a dirge now—without its soothing effect.*

AUTUMN 1861—GENERAL McCLELLAN APOLOGIZES

About the middle of August, there was a skirmish at Pohick Church, six miles below Mount Vernon. Northern pickets had been placed at Hollin Hall, north of Mount Vernon, while in the village of Accotink, just a short distance to the south, Confederate soldiers had arrested the mill owner and taken him to Richmond for questioning.

On October 3, the picket guard was recalled from Hollin Hall, and the Mount Vernon neighborhood quieted down temporarily. That very same day, Sarah was given a new pass, giving her access to Alexandria and Washington City.

Upon returning to Mount Vernon, Sarah discovered that the road to Alexandria had been blockaded. She waited until her pantry ran out of meat for the servants. Then she decided to take a back road to visit a neighbor three or four miles to the west. She wandered through the woods for hours until she found an alternate route to Washington City. She went to see General Scott, who was sick. Then she met Colonel Townsend, who suggested that she write down everything for General Scott. The general suggested that she see Mr. Lincoln, for if his pass was disputed, there was "no power but the president who could help me!"

So she went to see President Lincoln, and she was received kindly and given a note to present to General McClellan. The general received the note and proclaimed that a great mistake had been made by the volunteer officers. He offered to send provisions by steam tug. She received a more favorable pass from General Scott. In an October 9 letter, she confided to Mrs. Comegys:

> *I have found that as the path of duty has been made plain to me; God, who is the strength of the weak and confiding, has gone beside me, smoothing the rough places; and where the help of human friend was needed, placing the kind and willing in my way. The kind approval of yourself and husband, of our good Regent, and the other ladies is an admirable stimulate.*

A few nights after Sarah wrote this letter, a group of Confederate cavalrymen came charging up the road to Alexandria from the south. They were met at Accotink by Federal troops. Shots, shouts and commands rang out. The Quakers in the neighborhood sought shelter in their cellars. The skirmish lasted until dawn, when each group withdrew to its own line. Sounds of firing had been clearly heard at Mount Vernon four miles away, but no soldier entered the grounds.

MISS SARAH AND THE LIEUTENANT

In November, an event occurred that exhibited the hospitality of Sarah and Mount Vernon. A group of soldiers came to visit, including a Lieutenant Pomeroy of the Fifth Michigan, who had just recently been discharged from the hospital with congestive fever. Mr. Herbert found him under a tree, suffering from delirium. He brought him into the mansion. Sarah was in Alexandria. When she returned, she found the young officer in a blanket on the floor in a raging fever. A doctor and ambulance had been called for, and his friends wanted to move him back to their camp. Sarah proclaimed that he should not be moved, even if forty ambulances should come. He was cared for during four days at Mount Vernon, without a doctor seeing him. Then he was well enough to leave.

By that time, General Scott had retired, and hundreds of unruly soldiers were coming to the gates. Sarah and Mr. Herbert continued to charge them twenty-five cents to enter. Most of the enlisted men pleaded poverty and could not pay. As the year 1861 drew to a close, there were reports of another skirmish down the road at Pohick Church, the red brick edifice that had been attended by George Washington and George Mason. Everything of value had been stolen from the church, even the heavy white baptismal font. The roof leaked and windows were broken, but the old brick walls stood proudly upright.

This raid took place on November 12. The Second Michigan Volunteers were under the command of Brigadier General Heintzelman. One of those participating, Lieutenant Charles Haydon, expressed his outrage over the devastation wrought upon the church:

> At 8½ a.m. we reached the church 12 miles out. Pohick Church is a brick building built in 1773. Gen. Washington contributed to building it & was a frequent attendant. It has a very ancient look & one would suppose that it might be sacred enough to be secure. I have long known that the Mich. 2nd had no fear or reverence as a general thing for God or the places where he is worshipped but I had hoped that the memory of Gen. Washington might protect almost anything with which it was associated. I believe our soldiers would have torn the church down in 2 days. They were all over it in less than 10 minutes tearing off the ornaments, splitting the woodwork and pews, knocking the brick to pieces & everything else they could get at. They wanted pieces to carry away...A more absolute set of vandals than our men can not be found on the face of the earth. As true as I am living I believe they would steal Washington's coffin if they could get to it.

5

Woodlawn, the Quaker House and Hollin Hill

The 1840s were the era of the clipper ships. Many were built in Philadelphia, some by Quakers. One such Quaker shipbuilder was Joseph Gillingham. In 1846, he sought a new source of oak and other hardwoods and sent a group of Friends to locate a fresh supply. Starting in Norfolk, Virginia, they journeyed northward. Upon reaching Philadelphia, they reported that the area near the Accotink Creek, some nine miles south of Alexandria, was the finest available site.

Later that year, Joseph Gillingham and his son, Chalkley Gillingham, went to the area to begin negotiations for the purchase of the tract. On March 29, 1847, they purchased some two thousand acres of the Woodlawn Plantation from the titleholder, Lorenzo Lewis of Fairfax. They also purchased one thousand acres of the Mount Vernon estate. In December 1847, the first Quaker, Thomas Wright, arrived. He and his family took up residence in the Woodlawn mansion and began the work of setting up a Quaker community. Chalkley Gillingham purchased a farm of some two hundred acres.

The year 1848 saw the arrival of many Quaker families. A sawmill was built and started cutting timber in January 1848. Chalkley reported in his journal:

The saw mill and flour mill are doing good business. The land is divided, except as much as is needed about the mills. We now have a store, school, smith shop and Meeting and are raising fine crops of grain and hay. We find no difficulty in getting along without the use of slave labor. This was

Woodlawn Mansion. Part of the wooded area of Northern Virginia bought by Quakers before the Civil War.

one object in coming here, to establish a free labor colony in a slave state. It works quite well as we expected and the influence it events upon the laboring population [the black workers] *is very encouraging—elevating them to a much better condition than they were before our establishment went into operation. One woman visited the saw mill one day after viewing for some hours the different operations, raised her hands and exclaimed "God bless the Yankees! I wish more of them would come here. Now all our people can get work, which before they could not."*

A letter from John A. Washington in 1851, just a few years after the sale of Woodlawn to the Quakers, shows the attitude of many native Virginians toward blacks. He wrote to his wife:

If the Woodlawn Quakers are successful in their undertaking, of which there is little doubt, they will produce quite a revolution in our neighborhood, for others will unquestionably follow them, and in no distant date we will have a population around here very far superior to our present inhabitants. We shall eventually be obliged to send off our slaves and have recourse to white labour for the cultivation of our lands & in our domestic employments, and this change alone, when it can be effected, I firmly believe will benefit us beyond any present calculation.

The introduction of industrious and respectable people in the place of an ignorant slave and in some cases a more degraded white population will be followed by the division and improvement of farms, the formation of schools and a general diffusion of knowledge, and morality that can never otherwise take place in this region of our State. Added to this, I am fully persuaded that in less than ten years our lands will double in value.

What follows are some excerpts from Chalkley Gillingham's journal, which he kept until 1872. I concentrate here on his entries from 1861.

APRIL 21: We held a Conference at the house of David Walton to consider what course we should pursue, in the agitated and distracted state of things; with rebel soldiers coming and encamping all around us to attack the City of Washington. We felt we were in great danger, our families exposed to the marauding and merciless soldiers, whose business it was to tear down and destroy the government. We, being of Northern birth, would be likely objects of their vengeance. So we concluded to take our families north of Washington, until things assumed a different appearance here.

APRIL 22–23: In the morning I left the farm, with the wife and other females, for Sandy Spring, Maryland, about twenty miles north of Washington, & went to my old friend B. Hallowell's. The next day, our two sons & some of the neighboring young men and most of the families of the settlement left in a body, being about eight carriage loads; as much as they could get into their carriage or market wagon. They left some domestics to take charge in their absence; in some cases no one was left in charge. The young men left to keep from being forced into the rebellious army and the women left to keep out of the way of the army.

APRIL 25: Myself and family spent one day at Sandy Spring where we found the people in great alarm about the rebellion. The people of Baltimore were refusing to let the U.S. troops pass through Baltimore [the Baltimore Riots were on April 19] *or even over Maryland soil to protect the City of Washington. We all met in the evening and concluded to journey on towards Pennsylvania, leaving all behind us; not knowing if we should ever see our things again. We expected the stock of Cattle and Horses to be carried off by the rebel soldiers, and the buildings burned. The roads everywhere leading north were filled with refugees flying from the Southern Army. We arrived at Uniontown, Carroll County Maryland in the evening.*

APRIL 26: All the caravans, except myself, wife, daughter and little maid left for New Jersey. We remained behind to watch the progress of events in Virginia. The U.S. troops were not to be stopped from coming to Washington. They came by way of Annapolis and came so fast that the southern troops were never able to get to Washington.

APRIL 27–MAY 17: We remained in Maryland three weeks helping our friends attend to their farming business. The Southern troops gave up the idea of an immediate attack upon Washington City. Things appeared more quiet, and my oldest son returned from New Jersey at my request. We went back into Virginia to our home. Found all quiet but considerable suffering by having things carried off. Our cattle were driven off. We succeeded in getting them back again after twice visiting the [Fairfax] Court House village, 15 miles distant. We remained home ten days, when I returned to Maryland for my family and also attended the Quarterly Meeting held at Pipe Creek.

MAY 27: Immediately after Meeting, myself and family returned home. None of the other families had yet returned, except for a few of the men. On our arrival in Alexandria we found that Union troops had entered and taken possession. It had been in possession of the Southern soldiers when I went back to get my family. The Union troops did not extend a mile south of Alexandria, so we had to cross over the lines of the Union army and live outside the U.S. government. We remained in this way until October 15th, when the government picket guards were extended just beyond us to our Meeting House. During all that time we were alarmed continually by scouting parties of rebel troops coming into the neighborhood and carrying off men, horses, wagons and provisions.

JULY 21–22: This was the celebrated battle day at Bull Run and the first day of the week. All day at our place we heard the roar of the Cannon distinctly. While we sat in Meeting we heard the noise of war and the roar of battle, and on the next day, just before noon, we heard that the Union troops had all returned from the battle in a panic. I went to Alexandria to ascertain the result of things. We had supposed, in case the Federal troops had to retreat back to Alexandria, we would have to leave our homes very suddenly. When I arrived in Alexandria, I think I never witnessed such a profusion and confusion of soldiers—and nearly everyone mud to the knees. The Federal troops left the field just before night and proceeded immediately on foot, exhausted as they were, to Alexandria, without stopping for rest, traveling all night in the rain. Very few returned in any kind of order; everyone was left to get along by his own way and in every conceivable condition. The rebels were so exhausted, and lost so many men, that they never pursued the Union troops.

AUGUST 1: Military matters continue. Troops are constantly coming from the north at the rate of about a thousand per day, and every place for ten miles around Washington is covered with them. Wherever they are, devastation follows in their train. R.F. Roberts, a Friend and cousin to my wife, who lives on the west side of Alexandria, has a farm of about 100 acres. The troops have covered it completely and destroyed every fence on the place, except a few small enclosures around the buildings. In the country, half way to our place from Alexandria, the fences and timber are completely destroyed, and in many places the dwellings also. The rebel soldiers destroy the Union mens' dwellings & the Union soldiers the rebels' dwellings.

Compare the above with the excerpt from Anne Frobel's diary. Neither Northern nor Southern soldiers came across well in the writings of this Southern Lady (Frobel) and Northern Friend (Gillingham).

Hollin Hill is a few miles north of the Woodlawn estate. It was once part of the 13,000-acre plantation owned by George Mason, neighbor of George Washington and father of the Bill of Rights. The current property is owned and used by the Mount Vernon Unitarian Church. As part of the Quaker movement, in 1852, Mr. Edward C. Gibbs, a sea captain whose ships sailed between New Jersey and Liverpool, England, purchased Hollin Hall and 297 acres of land. Throughout the Civil War, the Gibbs family remained at Hollin Hall. Being Quakers, they took no part in the conflict, but the war nonetheless touched their lives. One afternoon, while out at the barn behind the house, a Confederate officer rode up and demanded that Edward Gibbs turn over to him a young black boy in his employ named Billy Holland. Mr. Gibbs complied, and the two rode off. It was not long before the officer returned to retrieve the boy's coat. Gibbs told him to go ahead into the barn to get it but to be careful, as Union pickets

Woodlawn Friends Meetinghouse—an island of peace in the no man's land between Federals and Confederates.

Federal soldier's graffiti (First Michigan Cavalry) is plainly visible on the outside boards of the Friends meetinghouse.

were on the nearby hill. At those words, the officer fled. Many years later, Charles Edward Gibbs, Edward Gibbs's son, who was with him during the episode, was a traveling machine salesman in the South. One evening, while staying with an elderly plantation owner, Charles began to talk about his war-time experience. His host, by strange coincidence, confessed to being that Confederate officer. He said that he had not been sent back for the boy's coat but instead had orders to burn the barn, where they believed that Yankee troops were being hidden. The threat of Union pickets on the hill had changed his mind, and the barn was spared. As for Billy Holland, he eventually made his way back to the area after the war and became an itinerant butcher, giving a good price on his meat to the Gibbs family. His descendants still live in the Gum Springs neighborhood.

In a letter dated July 1861, Elizabeth Troth Gibbs, Edward's wife, wrote to her brother in Philadelphia:

Hollin Hall has been invaded by desperadoes, deserters from both the North and the South, who have banded together to beg or steal food to survive. After being awakened from a sound sleep, I found food for the men, who repaid my kindness by stealing poultry and $10 worth of spoons and jewelry.

The Gibbs family remained at Hollin Hall until 1869. Two of the children born in the house still lived in Alexandria into the 1920s.

6

Fairfax Court House

Civil War Firsts

The city of Fairfax, with a current population of 22,500, celebrated its fiftieth anniversary in 2011 as an independent entity in the heart of Fairfax County. Today, it is famous as the home of George Mason University, one of Virginia's largest colleges, propelled to national fame as a Final Four Cinderella team in the NCAA March Madness in 2006. At the time of the Civil War, it was Fairfax Court House, a village of 300 souls, which for most of the latter part of 1861 served as the headquarters of the Confederate Army of the Potomac.

As the city of Alexandria was being taken over by Union forces on May 24, 1861, Fairfax Court House was under the command of Lieutenant Colonel Richard Ewell, Virginia Militia. He had arrived there on May 17. The militia under Ewell consisted of two hundred lightly armed men from the Prince William Cavalry, under Captain William W. Thornton; the Rappahannock Cavalry, under Captain John S. Green; and, arriving May 31, the Warrenton Rifles, under Captain John Quincy Marr. Their weapons included an assortment of personal arms, including flintlocks, and their primary duty was performing reconnaissance and picket duty. Additional militia was located about four miles south at Fairfax Station. Also arriving that day was former Virginia governor William "Extra Billy" Smith.

FIRST CONFEDERATE SOLDIER WOUNDED

On May 26, Privates Peyton Anderson and William Lillard were serving picket duty on Church Road (present-day Lee Highway near Fairfax Circle). Anderson made friends with eight-year-old Jimmie Walker, a boy who lived just north of his picket post. Suffering from hunger, he asked Jimmy if the boy's mother could send some breakfast the next morning. As promised, Jimmy was bringing food the next day when he was confronted by two horsemen, who asked if there were any soldiers in the area. Jimmie pointed out the location of Anderson and Lillard. The boy heard shots ring out and learned that Anderson had been shot and Lillard captured. Private Anderson was severely wounded in the arm and left at his post to die. He later revived, crawled to a nearby farmhouse and was taken to Fairfax for treatment. He was discharged in January 1862 and enlisted in Mosby's Rangers in 1864.

FIRST TROOP ENGAGEMENT, FIRST CONFEDERATE OFFICER KILLED

On the evening of May 31, Union lieutenant Charles Tompkins was in command of about eighty cavalry from Company B, Second U.S. Cavalry. At about 3:00 a.m. on June 1, they headed toward the courthouse. Captain Marr's pickets fired warning shots when the detachment was three-quarters of a mile from the town. Across the street from the courthouse was the Wilcoxon Hotel (James W. Jackson had been proprietor here before taking over the Marshall House in Alexandria). The Federals shot wildly into the hotel. They drove the Prince William Cavalry before them and captured several men. There was no Confederate return fire during the first Union charge.

Lieutenant Colonel Ewell came out of the hotel to re-form the Confederates. He was wearing his Virginia Militia uniform of dark blue, the same color as the Federals, so he discarded his frock coat. At first, the troops refused to listen to him—he had not been formally introduced. Then, Governor Smith attested to Ewell's authority and helped form the troops. The Federal cavalry reversed its course and came back through town. This time, they were met by Confederate gunfire. They escaped using a different route, having lost three troopers as prisoners and four horses killed.

A monument at Fairfax Court House dedicated to Captain John Quincy Marr, the first Confederate officer killed in the war.

Unbeknownst to all the participants, Captain Marr had been killed by a random shot. He was found in a clover field near the courthouse. The Federals reported that they had one killed, four wounded and one missing but had captured five Confederates. Lieutenant Tompkins was later reprimanded for his exaggerated claims, which appeared in the Northern papers. In 1893, General Charles Tompkins received the Medal of Honor for his unauthorized raid in 1861.

Outside the courthouse today stands a marker placed in 1904 by the Marr Camp of Confederate Veterans that reads: "This Stone Marks the Scene of the Opening Conflict of the War of 1861–1865, When John Q. Marr, Captain of the Warrenton Rifles, Was the First Soldier Killed in Action."

VIENNA—FIRST DESTRUCTION OF A TROOP TRAIN

Arriving later on June 1, overall Confederate commander P.G.T. Beauregard, the hero of Fort Sumter, observed the vulnerability of the local militia. He would need to protect the area with trained professional troops and extend them toward the enemy. Shortly thereafter, Colonel Maxcy Gregg's First South Carolina Infantry, a regiment of nearly 750 men, arrived from Richmond. They set up camp about three-quarters of a mile east, on the farm of Elisha Ostrander. A New Yorker who had come to Northern Virginia for the cheap land, Ostrander would later submit a damage claim to the U.S. government for destroying his land, fences and trees. In his claim, he stated that his land suffered no damage at the hands of the South Carolinians, whom he said brought their own firewood and supplies.

Gregg's force ranged as far as the Potomac River, about twelve miles to the northeast, with the village of Vienna halfway in between. By mid-June 1861, Falls Church was in Union hands, and Union troops were probing toward Leesburg and Winchester. Early on the morning of June 17, a detachment of 575 South Carolinians linked with the Fairfax Cavalry under Captain Edward Powell and a battery of six-pounder guns of the Alexandria Light Artillery under Captain Delaware Kemper. Returning from a long scout to the Potomac, the troops took up position along the rail line in Vienna, awaiting the arrival of Union troops, following a schedule they had done for two days. At 6:30 p.m., as Colonel Gregg was preparing to leave for the courthouse, he heard a train whistle and placed the two guns on a hill where they would intercept the train from four hundred yards. When the train came into the target area, it was raked with grape and canister from Kemper's Battery, inflicting serious damage and killing a number of Union soldiers.

The engine had been pushing the flatcars of Union troops. When the firing started, the engine was detached and steamed backward to Alexandria, leaving the embattled U.S. soldiers to fend for themselves. According to Colonel Gregg, his troops moved into the target area, capturing Union stragglers and burning the two remaining damaged cars, and then moved back to the courthouse. According to Brigadier General Robert Schenck, the local Union commander, in his report of June 18:

> *Total killed and wounded 12. None, I believe are now missing. From a reliable source I ascertain that the whole force attacking us was at least*

A lithograph of the first attack on a train as it moved troops during the Civil War.

2,000 as follows: South Carolina troops, 800; these had left Fairfax Court House and gone over to the railway; two hundred came down through Hunter's Grove...The enemy had cavalry, numbering, it is believed, not less than 200, and, in addition to these, a body of 150 armed picked negroes, who were observed by us, as they lay flat in the grain and did not fire a gun *[emphasis added]*.

Could this be the first instance of black Confederate troops?

Could these troops at Vienna have been one reason for the black abolitionist Frederick Douglass to state in his *Douglass' Monthly* in September 1861:

It is now pretty well established, that there are at the present moment many colored men in the Confederate army doing duty not only as cooks, servants and laborers, but as real soldiers, having muskets on their shoulders, and bullets in their pockets, ready to shoot down loyal troops, and do all that soldiers may to destroy the Federal Government and build up that of the traitors and rebels. There were such soldiers at Manassas.

Falls Church—First Balloon Reconnaissance

On June 24 occurred the first reconnaissance by observation balloon in the Civil War. The original aeronaut was Thaddeus Sobieski Coulincourt Lowe, aka Professor Lowe.

Professor Lowe was an aeronaut, scientist and inventor, mostly self-educated in the fields of chemistry, meteorology and aeronautics, and the father of military aerial reconnaissance in the United States. By the late 1850s, he was well known for his advanced theories in the meteorological sciences, as well as balloon building. Among his aspirations were plans for a transatlantic flight (such a flight had been written by Edgar Allan Poe in 1844 as *The Balloon Hoax*). Lowe's scientific endeavors were cut short by the onset of the war. He recognized his patriotic duty to the United States and offered his services as an aeronaut for the purposes of performing aerial reconnaissance on the Confederate troops on behalf of the Union army.

His participation in the war got off to a rocky start when he attempted a flight from Cincinnati, Ohio, to Washington City. For this flight, he used his smaller balloon *Enterprise*. His flight took off in the early morning of April 19, 1861, two days after Virginia had seceded. The air currents misdirected him to Unionville, South Carolina, where he was put under house arrest as a Yankee spy. Having established his identity as a man of science, he was allowed to return home, where he received word from Secretary of the Treasury Salmon P. Chase to come to Washington with his balloon. The war permanently ended Lowe's attempts at transatlantic flight.

On the evening of June 11, 1861, Lowe met President Lincoln, and on June 18, he performed a demonstration with the *Enterprise* at the present Federal Triangle in Washington. He sent a telegraph message from a height some five hundred feet above the White House. Lowe asserted:

> *This point of observation commands an area nearly fifteen miles in diameter. I have great pleasure in sending you this first dispatch ever telegraphed from an aerial station, and in acknowledging indebtedness to your encouragement, for the opportunity of demonstrating the availability of the science of aeronautics in the military service of the country.*

On June 22, Lowe filled his balloon at the Washington Gas Works (although erroneously called "hot air balloons" to this day, Lowe's balloons were held aloft by hydrogen gas) and, with the help of fifteen assistants, first walked his balloon up to Arlington House and then out to Taylor's Tavern in Falls Church, which was the extreme limit of Union control in Northern Virginia. On June 24, he made his first ascent, marking the first time in the war that a balloon was used to observe enemy forces. On June 25, he made several more ascents, during which new maps and good public relations were made. Following First Manassas, the area came back under Confederate control. On September 24, Lowe directed artillery by flag signals for the first time on massed Confederate troops in the Falls Church area who were celebrating the promotion of Colonel J.E.B. Stuart to brigadier general. The Rebels evacuated from the area two days later, and on September 29, Union troops reoccupied the Falls Church region for the remainder of the war.

Falls Church and its vicinity remained a no man's land throughout the summer and fall of 1861. One local resident, Timothy B. Munson, who before the war had run a nursery on Munson's Hill, had the following letter printed in the *Washington Evening Star* on August 10, 1861:

> *Editor* Star*: I am a resident of Fairfax County near Bailey's Crossroads, but have been compelled to stay here* [in Washington], *with the exception*

A lithograph of Professor Thaddeus Lowe's reconnaissance ascension from Falls Church, Virginia—the first use of aerial observation during the war. Ever since it has been called erroneously a hot air balloon, but it was actually filled with hydrogen gas.

of a few short intervals, since the war commenced. My son, during my absence, has had the care of my farm. If any doubt may arise as to my being a Union man, it may be sufficient for me to state that my vote last fall [November 1860] was cast for Abraham Lincoln, which has been the cause of my involuntary exile.

I wish to bring to your notice the fact that Federal troops have been recently committing the most wonton depredations upon my property, and the property of other Union men in the vicinity. They have already taken $200 worth of peaches from me, coming with the most unblushing impudence directly under the eye of my son, in broad daylight. Upon being remonstrated with, they reply "that their Colonel told them whenever they were short of provisions to help themselves wherever they find it."

One day this week during the absence of my son in Alexandria a party of soldiers came in the pasture, took a valuable farm horse, carried it into their camp, saying that they had taken a horse from a secessionist living outside of the lines. About the same time they shot one of my sheep and carried it off. Parties frequently come to the house and order dinner, without any show of politeness, and without any offer of compensation.

These depredations are committed mainly by the New York Thirty-seventh Regiment, Irish volunteers, stationed three miles this side of Alexandria.

My God! How long must these things continue? We may well exclaim, Save us from our friends!!!

By the end of August, there was such chaos that one Falls Church slave, Isaac Bennett, had escaped his master and entered Union picket lines near Ball's Crossroads (present Ballston). He reported that slaves everywhere were being impressed into Confederate service as soldiers; his uncle was serving as a soldier at Manassas.

FRONT LINE OF THE CONFEDERACY: JULY–OCTOBER 1861

From July 17 until July 23, Union forces under General Irwin McDowell were in control of Fairfax Court House, as they first surged toward their rendezvous with destiny at First Manassas (Bull Run) and then

General P.G.T. Beauregard. The fiery Creole, along with General "Stonewall" Jackson, wanted to take the fight to Washington, D.C., and end the war quickly. *Courtesy of Douglas Bostick.*

retreated back to Alexandria and Washington City. Colonel J.E.B. Stuart commanded the advance Confederate forces and reported, "I arrived and halted beyond the town at 9:30 p.m.…The enemy's operations may be known by the papers enclosed. The retreat continued in utter disorder into Washington City: 50,000 said to be engaged…Papers say there is no force this side of Alexandria; 50,000 [Union] men are to be mustered out of service in 15 days." Also on July 23, Colonel Hunton's Eighth Virginia regiment, with three companies of cavalry, was ordered separated for the reoccupation of Leesburg, and other forces were to reenter the Fairfax and Vienna area.

While General Beauregard was eager to follow up McDowell's defeat with a complete destruction of the Union army and end the war, he faced many weaknesses in his own forces. They lacked basic subsistence, transportation and arms, and many volunteers were coming to the end of their enlistment periods. Both the Union and Confederacy had called up ninety-day men, hoping that one quick battle would end the war. Beauregard worked hard to solve the logistical and morale problems, while his generals, such as James Longstreet, worked hard to locate and determine the strength and intent of the enemy. At least for the immediate future, Northern Virginia, except for the area immediately surrounding Alexandria, was under the control of Confederate forces—and Beauregard looked for ways to finish off the enemy and win independence for the Confederacy.

The future Partisan Ranger John Singleton Mosby, as a Confederate scout, had this to write to his wife about a week after First Manassas:

Fairfax Court House, July 29, 1861.

Dearest Pauline:

We have made no further advance and I know no more of contemplated movements than you do…A few nights ago we went down near Alexandria to stand as a picket (advance) guard. It was after dark. When riding along the road a volley was suddenly poured into us from a thick clump of pines. The balls whistled around us and Captain Jones' horse fell, shot through the head. We were perfectly helpless, as it was dark and they were concealed in the bushes. The best of it was that the Yankees shot three of their own men—thought they were ours…Beauregard has no idea of attacking Alexandria. When he attacks Washington he will go about Alexandria to attack Washington. No other news. For one week before the battle [First Manassas] we had an awful time—had about two meals during the whole time—marched two days and one night on one meal, in the rain, in order to arrive in time for the fight…We captured a great quantity of baggage left here by the Yankees; with orders for it to be forwarded to Richmond.

As a result of McDowell's defeat, President Lincoln called General George B. McClellan, the hero of Philippi (a Union victory in western Virginia on June 3, considered by some the first battle of the war), to Washington City to sort out the confusion and defend the capital. Arriving on July 26 to much fanfare and promise, McClellan found a disorganized and defeated army of fifty-two thousand and a city of politicians in panic. He remarked:

I found no preparations whatever for defense, not even to putting the troops in military position. A determined attack would doubtless have carried Arlington Heights and placed the city at the mercy of a battery of rifled guns. If the Secessionists attached any value to the possession of Washington, they committed their greatest error in not following up the victory of Bull Run.

On August 17, McDowell's Department of Northeastern (or Northern) Virginia was merged with the Department of Washington to become the new Department of the Potomac, better known as the Army of the Potomac. In a strange twist of fate, the legendary armies that faced each other from 1862 to 1865—the Confederate Army of Northern Virginia and the Union Army of the Potomac—were early in the war the Confederate Army of the Potomac and the Union Army of Northern Virginia!

"On to Washington!"

"On to Washington!" was now the cry of the Confederate press, just as before First Manassas "On to Richmond!" had been preached by the Northern press. And when there was no movement to follow McDowell into Washington City, who was to blame for not ending the war right then and there? While President Davis and Generals Beauregard and Johnston understood the limitations of the Confederate forces and their limited follow up, rumors filtered into the Southern press that each one was blaming the other. Especially Beauregard seemed culpable as he exhibited his natural frustration and impatience with not being able to carry the war to the opponent. Yet he remained resourceful, energetic and totally dedicated to the cause.

Recognizing that this assemblage of volunteers, militia and regulars were ill prepared for any sustained battle, Beauregard pleaded with Confederate commissary general Lucius B. Northrop for immediate supplies of food, shelter and medicines—but without success. On July 23, he appealed directly to President Davis and on July 29, to Colonels W.P. Miles and James Chesnut, who had acted as volunteer aids in South Carolina and Virginia and were both members of the Confederate Congress.

By the beginning of August, Beauregard had finally received some relief and moved to extend his army forward and formulate plans for an offensive. On August 8, he ordered Colonel Nathan Evans to march his entire brigade into the Leesburg area and extend his control of Loudoun County. Colonel Hunton was reunited with his old brigade under the command of Evans.

On August 10, under Beauregard's orders, Longstreet's brigade began relocating to the courthouse. Colonel Stuart's cavalry headquarters were nearby, and he might have quartered in the Ford House (presently law offices about half a block from the old courthouse), where he befriended their daughter Antonia. As Beauregard repositioned his forces, General Joseph Johnston balked at advancing too far forward toward Washington; the conservative Johnston outranked Beauregard but did comply with some of his suggestions. The two generals, though always cordial, often reflected their differences in personality while formulating military tactics. The aggressive Beauregard favored subjecting an adversary's movements to his own plans, while Johnston, ever on the defensive, sought to react to the action of the enemy. In spite of these differences in personality, they had a fond respect for each other, and Johnston's defensive nature served as a check on the

General Joseph Johnston. He was overall in charge of Confederate forces during and after First Manassas. He supported a slow and serious response to Northern aggression. *Courtesy of the Library of Congress.*

brashness of Beauregard. They were more effective as a team then either one would have been on his own.

Beauregard instructed Colonel Stuart to stay close to the enemy and General Longstreet, with his brigade, to stay close to Stuart. By the end of August, Stuart, together with Longstreet, had captured Mason's and Munson's Hills, and Confederate forces were in full view of Washington. Union forces made a demonstration to retake the hills but were driven back by Longstreet's forces. This led to the establishment of an important Rebel observation post on Mason's Hill from which Beauregard was to receive information about the activities of McClellan in Washington. Longstreet held this position until late September, when Southern forces were pulled back to Fairfax Court House.

According to the Confederates, many of the local citizens suffered severely from the time when the area was in the control of the Federals. The Ball House, owned by cavalry Captain Ball, who was captured with his troopers in Alexandria at the beginning of the war, had been spitefully damaged. Union troops had broken doors and windows, broke open and robbed trunks and wardrobes, smashed mirrors and did not leave a whole piece of furniture in the house.

On orders from Beauregard, signal officer Captain E.P. Alexander set about to establish communications between informants in Washington City and Mason and Munson Hills. (During First Manassas, Alexander had delivered the message to Colonel Evans: "Look to your left, you are turned," indicating that Evans was going to be flanked on his left. Evans prevented this, thus saving his regiment. After the battle, General Beauregard was pleased and impressed with Alexander and the Signal Corps. Alexander has the distinct honor of being the first to send a signal by the aerial telegraphy method during the war.) Communications were already in place between Mason Hill and the courthouse.

Captain E. Pliny Bryan, CSA, a former member of the Maryland General Assembly that had sought secession in that state, was Alexander's contact in Washington. Bryan had a hotel room in Georgetown that Porter could see from Mason Hill with his six-foot telescope. Bryan would signal him with a coffee pot reflecting the sun or movement of the window drapes. Response from the hill was by way of giant flags and firing cannons. This system was used until mid-October, when the Confederates began deploying to Centreville for winter quarters.

J.E.B. Stuart also used the hills to intimidate and mislead the enemy. He placed fake wooden cannons (Quaker guns) painted black so that at a distance they resembled real guns and paraded men around large campfires at night to lead the Federals into believing they were heavily fortified and highly manned.

Early in September, in response to a display of rockets by the enemy, Beauregard ordered Captain Alexander to set off a large display of rockets along the entire Confederate line from Occoquan on the right to the Potomac north of Falls Church on the left, a distance of ten miles. Observing this in

Washington City, the people assumed that McClellan was advancing that night, and the Confederates showed their willingness to engage.

On September 6, Beauregard proposed to advance his front line forward so the enemy could be effectively engaged near Falls Church. He suggested placing five brigades on and around the Falls Church hills, two brigades near Annandale and one brigade each near Springfield and present-day Tyson's Corner, with reserves near the courthouse. The move was opposed by General Johnston, who believed the army was already too far advanced toward Washington City. On September 12, Beauregard moved his headquarters in Fairfax to the former Ratcliffe Mansion, which had briefly served as headquarters for Union General McDowell and would later serve as headquarters for General McClellan.

BIRTHPLACE OF THE CONFEDERATE BATTLE FLAG

General Beauregard, with support and encouragement of Johnston and other generals, had been seeking a distinctive new Confederate flag approved for use in the field. The similarity between the Stars and Stripes and the Stars and Bars had created anxious moments and near disasters during First Manassas. Beauregard had some concepts for a new flag, as had others, but the final decision closely followed a design proposed earlier by Colonels William P. Miles and J.B. Walton, based on a design developed by Edward Hancock of New Orleans.

Beauregard first sought to have the Confederate national flag changed from the Stars and Bars, and he sought the assistance of Miles, chairman of the Confederate House Military Committee. Miles had served on Beauregard's staff in Charleston, South Carolina. At his request, a report was written recommending a change, but the proposal failed by a four-to-one vote; the lone yea vote was that of Miles. On September 5, Beauregard wrote to Johnston, "How would it do for us to address the War Department on the subject for a supply of regimental, war, or badge flags, made of red with two blue bars crossing each other diagonally, on which shall be introduced stars…We would then, on the field of battle, know our friends from our enemies."

General W.L. Cabell, chief quartermaster of the Confederate army in Virginia, recalled the meeting held at Beauregard's headquarters in Fairfax when the final design of the flag was agreed upon. Prior to this meeting, Colonel Walton had met with Beauregard and Johnston and supplied several designs for consideration. Also, it appears that both Johnston and Beauregard had their draftsmen draw up several candidates. While there were some differences, there was a great deal of similarity in regard to the basic colors, the St. Andrews cross (the national flag of Scotland) and the use of stars. General Cabell recalled in 1900 that he was summoned by telegraph to come immediately to Fairfax Court House for the meeting with Beauregard and Johnston.

He recalled that both Beauregard and Johnston were in Beauregard's office discussing the kind of flag that should be adopted. Johnston's design was in the shape of an ellipse, a red flag with a blue St. Andrews cross, with white stars on the cross to represent the different Southern states and no borders. Beauregard's was a rectangle with a blue St. Andrews cross and white stars, similar to Johnston's. After examination and discussion, it was decided that an elliptical flag would be too hard to make, so Beauregard's was accepted. But there is also evidence that the design approved was actually square rather than rectangular. The design was submitted to the War Department and approved.

The Cary sisters of Baltimore and Alexandria were given the honor by the Committee of Congress of making the first three Confederate battle flags. After finishing their work, they were allowed to add a gold fringe to each flag and present them to their favorite general. Hetty's flag was presented to General Johnston and Connie's to General Earl Van Dorn. Both flags are in the Museum of the Confederacy. Jennie's flag went to General Beauregard and is now in New Orleans. The flag was supposed to come in three sizes: forty-eight inches square for infantry units, thirty-six inches square for artillery units and thirty inches square for cavalry.

The original battle flags carried twelve stars rather than the thirteen usually seen in present-day representations. It is believed that the twelve stars represented each of the eleven seceding states, plus one star for Maryland, which the sisters believed had been prevented from seceding when Lincoln jailed its General Assembly. The Cary sisters, two being from Maryland, might have added the twelfth star of their own volition.

Later, a thirteenth star was added to the center to represent the states of Kentucky, Missouri and New Mexico Territory, which sent troops to serve the Confederacy although they never actually seceded. The thirteen-star version of the battle flag later became part of the second and third Confederate national flags.

The generals ordered 120 silk battle flags for issue to the army. Quartermaster Colin M. Selph bought the entire silk supply of Richmond

The original Confederate battle flag was square. Still a contentious symbol, General Beauregard had it designed while headquartered at Fairfax Court House because the official Confederate national flag too closely resembled the Stars and Stripes.

for making the flags (and the only red-like colors available in bulk were either pink or rose, hence these flags were of lighter shades). The flag making was contracted to some Richmond sewing circles. In lieu of gold fringe, a silk yellow border was used, as was a blue hoist sleeve for the flagpole.

Starting in late November 1861, the new battle flags were presented to the Confederate units at Centreville, and into December, they went to other units in nearby parts of Northern Virginia. The flags were presented to each regiment by Generals Beauregard and Johnston, as well as other army officers, in elaborate parade ground affairs.

A *Richmond Whig* newspaper article of December 2, 1861, tells of the presentation at Centreville on November 28:

> *The exercises were opened by Adjutant General Jordan, who, in a brief but eloquent address, charged the men to preserve from dishonor the flags committed to their keeping. The officers then dismounted and the colonels of the different regiments coming forward to the center, Gen. Beauregard, in a few remarks, presented each with a banner, and was eloquently responded to. The regiments then came to "present," and received their flags with deafening cheers.*

PRESIDENT JEFFERSON DAVIS'S WAR COUNCIL

Without doubt, the most historic event ever to occur at Fairfax Court House was the visit by President Jefferson Davis from September 30 through October 3, 1861. During his visit was held probably the most important military strategy meeting of the war. Some Civil War historians say that the errors made at this conference led to the Confederacy's eventual defeat. The conference was followed by a formal review of the troops and then a magnificent parade—possibly the largest presidential review and parade ever held by the Confederacy.

Although festive on the surface, divergence of opinions regarding a workable defensive strategy for the Confederacy had been brewing for months, and strong differences in personalities would play out in the discussions that followed. Two weeks prior to Davis's visit, he had expressed deep-seated dissatisfaction with General Johnston. But he was also uncomfortable with the aggressive nature of General Beauregard, relying on Johnston to keep Beauregard in check. Strategically, however, the question was whether victory could be best attained by remaining defensive, continually inflicting damage on the Union and finally wearing it down, or by going on the offensive, striking the Union and capturing important cities like Washington, Baltimore and Philadelphia, hoping this would lead to peace. Beauregard favored the latter while Davis consistently held that the Union would tire of war and leave the Confederacy to live in peace. This issue would need to be decided as the Confederacy prepared for McClelland's expected attack before winter set in.

   While the troops expected a Union invasion across the Falls Church hills, the generals expected a flanking movement, either upstream near Leesburg or downstream near Dumfries. But the ever-aggressive Beauregard had devised a plan for a decisive battle, the result of which would be to either win or lose the battle for independence. He had even managed to persuade the defensive-minded Johnston and newly arrived General Gustavus W. Smith. They preferred a bold but risky offensive move to the certainty of unrest, dissension and sickness of troops wintering in idleness. In order to do this, they would need an urgent concentration of troops from all parts of Virginia and beyond. Thus, General Smith recommended an urgent meeting with the president.

   Beauregard's plan was to raise the troop level from near forty thousand to sixty thousand by drawing troops from various parts of the Confederacy, replacing them with six-month state militias. The main force would cross the Potomac either near Leesburg or just north of the courthouse. This force would march on Washington City and seize the Federal supplies there. If McClellan reached the threatened point in time, he could not withstand the attack and maintain his position. The assessment was that the Union forces were undisciplined, still demoralized from First Manassas and could easily be defeated by the Confederate forces, also winning Maryland over to the Rebel side. This would thus transfer the main theater of war to the Northeast and relieve attacks expected along the Mississippi River. The impact of such an exhibition of Confederate power might then cause the governments of Great Britain and France to enter on the side of the Confederacy, as had been their leaning and as would be to their economic benefit due to their need for cotton, which in 1860 had been the main export of the United States.

   Although the topic of military posturing had been discussed constantly with the War Department in Richmond, the generals sought a Conference of War at the very highest level. General Johnston prepared the formal request on September 26, addressing it to recently installed Secretary of War Judah Benjamin (the first Jewish cabinet member in American history). He asked for a direct conference with His Excellency, the president, or the secretary of war. The proposed offensive action went far beyond Davis's past defensive orders, but he agreed to meet for this conference, during which a new course could be set for the Confederate government. The proceedings of this meeting have been examined by military historians who believe that Davis's failure to switch to an offensive mode was the pivotal decision of the war. The meeting is recorded in history as President Davis's Fairfax Court House Conference.

Confederate president Jefferson Davis. He visited Fairfax Court House in October 1861 for a Council of War to discuss how best to win Southern independence.

Whether President Davis entered the conference with an open mind or grasped it as an opportunity to personally assess the situation at Fairfax and acquaint the generals with the realities of the limitations of his government is still a matter of conjecture. He did leave Richmond at 6:00 a.m. on September 30 and arrived at Fairfax Station that evening, with a brief stop at Manassas Junction. He was greeted by Generals Johnston, Beauregard and Smith, who escorted him up to the courthouse amidst throngs of cheering troops and citizens. After a brief reception at General Beauregard's headquarters, Davis asked Johnston and Smith to join him there the next evening, October 1, at 8:00 p.m., for the important discussions that were the purpose of his trip.

The conference commenced at 8:00 p.m., as scheduled, on October 1 and ended about midnight. A transcript of the proceedings was kept by General

Smith and is contained in the *Official Records of the War of the Rebellion*, volume five. President Davis was not aware that the proceeding was being recorded and reacted angrily when told of this years later. The discussion continued for hours, with Davis noting his inability to meet the needs in other theaters of operation and the generals recounting that concentration and success in the Washington region would cause the Federals to pull back forces from other areas to protect the Northern states. Of course, the president was responsible for protecting the entire Confederacy.

Reviewing Beauregard's plan, Davis asked how many "seasoned" troops would be necessary for its success. The general replied that sixty thousand men would be necessary, requiring large additional transportation and munitions, their present supplies being entirely inadequate for any active campaign under present conditions. The president responded with surprise and regret that the number of surplus arms was so small there and that no reinforcements could be furnished of the type asked for. The most he could send was twenty-five hundred recruits to use the arms they had at hand. The whole country was praying and demanding protection. He was hoping to receive arms from abroad, but nothing had materialized. Manufacture of arms locally in the Confederacy had not been implemented yet. Want of arms was the final problem, and because of that, he could not bring in extra soldiers.

The morning of October 3 brought clearing skies, and by noon, the grand salute to Davis would take place, the disappointment of the generals having been set aside. The troops were lined up about a mile and a half west along Little River Turnpike, starting from the Wilcoxon Hotel across from the courthouse. President Davis and the generals rode past the line of troops, saluting each flag as they passed them, and then returned to a reviewing stand, probably at the hotel. After a review, parade and reception, Davis was escorted back to Fairfax Station, and his train headed back to Richmond.

It was left to "Stonewall" Jackson to devise a plan for invading the North and show exactly what it could accomplish. In mid-October, a week after he had been promoted to major general and named to command the forces in the Shenandoah Valley, Jackson visited General Smith in his tent at the courthouse. Smith had also been promoted to major general, commanding a division of the army. Jackson told Smith:

> *McClellan, with his army of recruits, will not attempt to come out against us this autumn. If we remain inactive, they will greatly have the advantage over us next spring. Their raw recruits will have become an organized army, vastly*

superior in numbers to our own. We are ready at the present moment for active operations in the field, while they are not. We ought to invade their country now, and not wait for them to make the necessary preparations to invade ours. If the president would reinforce this army by taking troops from other points not threatened, and let us make an active campaign of invasion before winter sets in, McClellan's raw recruits will not stand against us in the field.

Crossing the upper Potomac, occupying Baltimore, and taking possession of Maryland, we could cut off the communications of Washington, force the Federal government to abandon the capital, beat McClellan's army if it came out against us in the open country, destroy industrial establishments wherever we found them, break up the lines of interior commercial intercourse, close the coal mines, seize and if necessary, destroy the manufactories and commerce of Philadelphia, and of other large cities within our reach; take and hold the narrow neck of country between Pittsburgh and Lake Erie; subsist mainly on the country we traverse, and making unrelenting war amidst their homes, force the people of the North to understand what it will cost them to hold the South in the Union at the bayonet's point.

Jackson asked Smith to use his influence with Johnston and Beauregard in favor of immediate aggressive operations. Smith responded that he had been present at the meeting at Fairfax just a few weeks prior, when the two generals had proposed an invasion of the North, and the president had rejected it. There was nothing he could do, Smith said.

Jackson rose from the ground where he had been sitting, shook Smith's hand warmly and said, "I am sorry, very sorry." Without another word, he went to his horse and rode sadly away.

BIRTH OF "THE BATTLE HYMN OF THE REPUBLIC"

Inspired by the Review at Upton's Hill

On November 18, Julia Ward Howe, with her husband, Dr. Samuel Gridley Howe, and a few friends, traveled to Upton's Hill in Falls Church to observe a review of Federal troops. Packed for the outing was an enormous hamper of fried chicken, Virginia ham, bottles of champagne and other delicacies for a very special picnic. They all sang "John Brown's Body" and several other Union marching tunes.

Julia Ward Howe. Her viewing of a Union army review in Northern Virginia inspired her to write "The Battle Hymn of the Republic."

The review had to be abruptly interrupted due to a military demonstration by nearby Confederates. The Howes, along with a few others, made their way back to Washington City and the Willard Hotel. By the next morning, Julia Howe had written the words to the "The Battle Hymn of the Republic" on the letterhead of the U.S. Sanitary Commission. The commission was the forerunner of the Red Cross. Howe remembered how she wrote it:

I went to bed that night as usual, and slept, according to my wont, quite soundly. I awoke in the gray of the morning twilight; and as I lay waiting for the dawn, the long lines of the desired poem began to twine themselves in my mind. Having thought out all the stanzas, I said to myself, "I must get up and write these verses down, lest I fall asleep again and forget them." So, with a sudden effort, I sprang out of bed, and found in the dimness an old stump of a pen which I remembered to have used the day before. I scrawled the verses almost without looking at the paper.

Mine eyes have seen the glory of the coming of the Lord:
He is trampling out the vintage where the grapes of wrath are stored;
He hath loosed the fateful lightning of His terrible swift sword:
His truth is marching on...
I have seen Him in the watch-fires of a hundred circling camps,
They have builded Him an altar in the evening dews and damps;
I can read His righteous sentence by the dim and flaring lamps:
His day is marching on.
(Chorus)
Glory, glory, hallelujah!
Glory, glory, hallelujah!
Glory, glory, hallelujah!
While God is marching on.

The song was published in the *Atlantic Monthly* in February 1862 and had an almost magical effect. It appeared that tired and hungry soldiers had their spirits lifted by singing "The Battle Hymn," as if a heavenly ally were descending with a song of succor, and thereafter the wet, aching marchers thought less of their wretched selves and thought more of their cause, their families and their country.

THE GRAND REVIEW AT BAILEY'S CROSSROADS

On November 20, between Munson's Hill and Bailey's Crossroads, General McClellan conducted the most impressive military review of his career. By all contemporary accounts, the weather had dramatically changed to cold, wintry conditions. Private Robert K. Sneden of E Company, Fortieth New York Volunteers (Mozart Regiment), described leaving his camp at Fort Ward near Alexandria at 5:00 a.m. to participate in the grand review. Playing bands and waving flags accompanied the soldiers. Their pride was evident in their polished brass buttons and gleaming guns. Sneden described their arrival at Bailey's Cross Roads in vivid terms:

> *It was a fine, though cold and windy day. Patches of snow were on the ground when we arrived there about 10:00 a.m., which made it muddy in places. Many regiments had overcoats on the men. Ours had not as the colonel wanted to show off the fine uniforms. The brigades were drawn up in columns while General McClellan and staff with President Lincoln rode up and down the lines while the bands played and a battery fired salutes.*
>
> *The heavy and light artillery with cannon polished like gold, and the ugly looking Parrot guns were drawn up in a long line, while the cavalry were massed in squadrons. Then about 2:00 p.m. all marched past in review. About half of the men had to stand in the cold wind for hours. Nearly everyone was thoroughly chilled. Many soon filled up the camp hospitals.*
>
> *The President with his bodyguard was cheered from end to end of the long lines of troops. The review lasted until 5 p.m. and all were not off the ground until darkness had set in. As the men had brought no rations and had been up and marching since five in the morning, all were hungry, thirsty and cold. They got to camp much quicker than on going out to the review. They were all much elated and no one ever can forget the splendid military*

President Abraham Lincoln and members of his cabinet came to Bailey's Crossroads in November to experience the grand review of the Federal army under General George B. McClellan.

sight it afforded. All the cooks in camp were at work for half of the night when we returned at 7 p.m. in a drizzling rain.

The troops on review must have made an impressive show. They were well trained and drilled. According to one soldier at Falls Church at that time, "The first thing in the morning is drill, then drill again. Then drill, drill, and a little more drill. Then drill and lastly drill. Between drills, we drill and sometimes stop to eat a little and have a roll-call."

A Wisconsin officer gave a firsthand account in a letter home:

On Tuesday we marched out to Bailey's Cross Roads to take part in the grand review...You know it was the largest review of troops ever in America, that 60,000 infantry, 9,000 cavalry, and 130 pieces of artillery passed in review before McClellan...that it took from 11 o'clock A.M. until 4 P.M. to pass the reviewing officer, and that the President, the members of the Cabinet, and all the celebrities, foreign and domestic, were present.

Another soldier confided an inside secret during the march:

We were no exception to the generality of mankind, of liking to see a pretty face, even if it did belong to a woman of secesh sentiments. When the boys at the head of the column discovered a pretty girl, if she was on the right side of the road, guide right would be passed along the line; and guide left if on the left side of the road. By this ingenious device we were enabled to direct our eyes where we would receive the largest return for our admiration.

THE FIRST EXCLUSIVELY MILITARY RAILROAD

The Centreville Military Railroad was a 5.5-mile spur running from the O&A Railroad east of Manassas Junction across Bull Run and up the south side of the Centreville Plateau. Built by the Confederate army between November 1861 and February 1862, it was the first exclusively military railroad.

General Johnston faced a Federal force superior in size, while his own Confederate army was spread thinly across central Fairfax County. To prepare a better defensible position, he concentrated his troops on the Centreville Plateau, the high ground between Little Rocky Run and Bull Run along the western edge of Fairfax County, with his main supply base at the Manassas Junction in his rear in Prince William County. The Centreville Plateau is located about six miles north of Manassas Junction in modern Manassas. The Confederates built an elaborate series of connected forts and military positions, and the Confederate cavalry and advanced pickets controlled the countryside as far east as Fairfax Court House.

The army went into camp and built winter quarters in Centreville that were protected by strong fortifications. The logistics of supplying forty thousand Confederate troops on the front lines grew worse with wet weather in October, so they withdrew even more into Centreville. Behind the lines, warehouses were built at Manassas Junction. Chapman (Beverly) Mill in Thoroughfare Gap, at the border of Prince William and Fauquier Counties, also served as a supply depot. Over one million pounds of meat were stored there in the winter of 1861–62 to feed the Rebel army.

The idea of building a railroad, using spare and captured parts, became a viable option to ox carts and wagon teams on the muddy Centreville Road. However, on November 7, the O&A disapproved a request to use any of

C 17

MILITARY
RAILROAD TERMINUS

Half a mile west is the terminus of the Centreville Military Railroad, the first railroad in the world constructed exclusively for military purposes. Built by the Confederate army late in 1861 because of impassable roads, it supplied the soldiers in their winter camps at Centreville. Trains from Manassas Junction ran here until March 1862 when Confederate forces withdrew southward. Nearby on 9 Dec. 1862, Privates Michael O'Brien and Dennis Corcoran of Maj. Chatham R. Wheat's "Louisiana Tigers" were court-martialed for mutiny, executed by a firing squad from their own company, and buried. In 1979 their remains were reinterred at St. John's Episcopal Church cemetery in Centreville.

Historical signage for the first exclusively military railroad, constructed by Confederates between Manassas Junction and Centreville.

its rails to build such a line. Private McClellan of the Ninth Alabama Infantry Regiment commented in his diary on November 23 that fifty thousand men were working on a six-mile railroad in shifts of six hours per day, causing them to have no time for working on winter huts. By November 30, newspaper articles reported that two months would be necessary to build the planned railroad.

Construction began in December from the O&A tracks at Manassas Junction. The new line was fully surveyed, was being leveled and would run four miles to Bull Run and then two miles beyond that to the rear of the army. The rails were brought in from warehouses, where they were being held in storage in Winchester, by wagon down to Strasburg and then by rail car to Manassas Junction. "It is no mystery that the iron for the track came from the South's one unfailing source of supply in 1861, the Baltimore and Ohio [B&O] Railroad," reported a deserter from the Sixth Louisiana Infantry, who left Centreville on January 7, 1862. The Pinkerton National Detective Agency confirmed on January 27, 1862, based on the report of another deserter, that the railroad construction was in progress.

Trains, pressed into service from the O&A ran on the line from Manassas Junction from about the second week of February 1862 until March 11, 1862, when Confederate forces withdrew southward. While the railroad was exclusively designed only for resupply of the army on a temporary and light track, an issue soon arose about the transportation of heavier loads of sick soldiers. Initially, the locomotives used were underpowered for hauling large loads of sick soldiers, and General Johnston did not allow use of the trains for transporting the sick. Later, larger locomotives were brought in, and Johnston changed his mind, allowing evacuations of the sick south to the large Confederate hospital located in Charlottesville. The O&A disagreed with Johnston's decision and actions but was overridden by order of Johnston to Major Barber to transport the sick all the way to Charlottesville.

Federal soldiers examining the earthworks from a distance came to believe that the defenses at Centreville were virtually impregnable. The Confederate defense line along Bull Run appeared too strong to General McClellan. He identified another route to Richmond that would bypass the Bull Run defenses: sail the Union army down the Potomac River to Fortress Monroe and then march up the peninsula past Williamsburg to Richmond.

The operation of the railroad was very short-lived, as General Johnston decided on March 9, 1862, to abandon his defensive positions on the Centreville Plateau and move south of the Rappahannock River to counter McClellan's movements to Hampton Roads. On March 11, 1862, the Confederates quickly abandoned their positions, tore up as much track as possible, leaving much of the rail lying in place, and destroyed the trestle bridge across Bull Run. Federal troops entered and occupied the area on that same day and decided to rip up and use the slightly worn rails for repairs elsewhere in Virginia.

FIRST EXECUTIONS DUE TO MUTINY

In November 1861, General Richard Taylor was challenged by General Johnston to whip his Louisianans, especially Wheat's seemingly out-of-control Tigers, into shape. The "Louisiana Tigers" was the common nickname for certain infantry troops from Louisiana in the Confederate army. Although it originally applied to a specific company, the nickname expanded to a battalion, then to a brigade and eventually to all Louisiana troops within the Confederate Army of the Potomac. Although the exact composition of the Louisiana Tigers changed as the war progressed, they developed a reputation as fearless, hard-fighting shock troops.

The origin of the term came from the "Tiger Rifles," a volunteer company raised in the New Orleans area as part of Major Chatham R. Wheat's First Special Battalion, Louisiana Volunteer Infantry (Second Louisiana Battalion). Major Wheat was born on April 9, 1826, in Alexandria, Virginia, to the Reverend John Thomas and Selina Blair Patten Wheat. As a boy, Wheat followed his father's Episcopal parsonages to Anne Arundel County, Maryland; Wheeling, Virginia; Marietta, Ohio; New Orleans, Louisiana; and Nashville, Tennessee. When he was fifteen, Wheat was sent back to Alexandria to study under the Reverend William Nelson Pendleton, a West

Point graduate, former U.S. Army officer and future artillery chief of Robert E. Lee's Army of Northern Virginia.

A large number of Wheat's men were foreign born, particularly Irish Americans, many from the New Orleans wharves and docks. Many men had previous military experience in local militia units or as mercenaries.

Originally, Company B of Wheat's Tigers wore the distinctive Zouave uniforms, with straw hats or red cloth fezzes, blue-striped pantaloons and short, dark blue jackets with red lacing. The Tiger Zouaves apparently wore the fezzes in camp and straw hats while on the battlefield. As time went on, this garb was replaced by Confederate uniforms and what clothing the men could purchase or otherwise obtain from civilians. Within months of arriving in Northern Virginia, Wheat's entire five-company battalion began to be called the Louisiana Tigers.

The battalion first saw combat at First Manassas, where it anchored the left flank on Matthews Hill for several hours until reinforcements arrived. During this action, the Tiger Battalion conducted several brazen attacks, with Colonel Wheat himself suffering a major wound.

With the Federal rout at Manassas, the men of the Special Battalion were able to supplement their Louisiana-made equipment with Yankee-made packs, blankets, gum blankets, canteens and haversacks that were discarded during their retreat. One reporter from the *New Orleans Daily Delta*, for example, stated, "[I noticed] that the knapsacks and haversacks of our Bengalese friends were all marked in large letter 'U.S.' I inquired what the letters meant. 'A few weeks ago,' was the ready reply, 'they meant 'Uncle Sam,' now they mean 'us.'"

By the fall of 1861, the Tigers were stationed with other Confederate troops in and about Centreville. It was General Johnston's desire to whip the Louisianans into military shape. To do so, Johnston promised to support General Taylor *in any measures to enforce discipline*. On November 28, just a few days after Taylor's elevation (some complained that it was simply because he was the son of former president Zachary Taylor), a gang of drunken Zouaves from the Tiger Rifles, apparently led by Privates Dennis Corcoran and Michael O'Brien, made the terrible mistake of testing Taylor's resolve when they attacked the brigade stockade, knocking the officer on duty to the ground and seizing the guards' weapons. The mob then proceeded to break fellow Tiger John Travers, who was being held on a murder charge, out of the jail. During the scuffle, one of the Zouaves reportedly struck Colonel Harry Hays of the Seventh Louisiana. Enraged, several other men of the brigade, who had had it with the Tigers, quickly squashed the riot, and

Corcoran, O'Brien and their Tiger brethren were subsequently arrested and thrown into the stockade to await trial.

This little episode led to the first executions in the Confederate Army of the Potomac. In an effort to enforce discipline, the government had given general court-martials the power to execute soldiers convicted of capital crimes such as murder, treason or mutiny. Taylor, as well as most of the other officers of the brigade who were sick and tired of the depraved activities of the Tigers, agreed that Corcoran and O'Brien were among the more caustic men of the battalion, if not the whole army, and decided to make an example of them. Because the riot at the guard house and Hays's subsequent thrashing were considered to be acts of mutiny, the two men were court-martialed the next day, November 29, found guilty and sentenced to be shot by members of their own company, "for the sake of the example."

The highly publicized execution took place a week later, on December 9, 1861, in a little hollow or depression forming a natural amphitheater, upon the slopes of which a vast multitude of soldiers assembled at 10:00 a.m. It was witnessed by Ewell's entire division, which was drawn up on three sides of a hollow square, facing inward, with Taylor's brigade in the center, Elzey's on the right and Trimble's on the left. Members of the press and other onlookers watched from vantage points in some trees or surrounding hills. Once the division was formed, a covered wagon, escorted by two companies from Colonel Henry Kelly's Eighth Louisiana Regiment, slowly drove into the open portion of the square, where it stopped in front of two large stakes driven into the ground about ten feet apart. Beside the stakes were two plain wooden coffins and matching grave sites, stark reminders of the business at hand. Soon after the wagon stopped, six men got out: Corcoran and O'Brien, still in their distinctive bleached Tiger Zouave uniforms; a Catholic priest, Father Smoulders of the Eighth Regiment; and three officers. At the same time, twenty-four men from the Tiger Rifles marched forward toward the stakes that were awaiting their occupants.

There had been some reason to suspect that the firing squad of the Tigers, as detailed, would at the critical moment disobey orders and refuse to fire on their comrades. To meet this contingency, Colonel Kelly had his men load their guns in camp before marching. Why this was done they never knew, only they thought it was a matter of course somehow at an execution. This trusted company merely happened to take position immediately to the rear of the firing party of Tigers, their captain with the secret orders to fire on them should they prove mutinous and fail to fire.

Gravestone for Privates Michael O'Brien and Dennis Corcoran in Saint John's Cemetery in Centreville, Virginia. They were the first members of the Confederate Army in Northern Virginia executed for mutiny.

All doubts were removed, however, when Lieutenant Adrian, who was wearing a long scarlet tunic, dryly hammered out the appropriate commands of "Ready, Aim, and Fire!" In the subsequent volley, Corcoran and O'Brien were killed instantaneously, falling forward on their knees, riddled with bullets. Once the bodies were cut away from the posts and loaded into the coffins, they were lowered into their graves and covered up. Afterward, some curious soldiers combed the execution site for pieces of the stakes or other macabre relics until some men from the Star Battalion angrily dispersed the foragers with fixed bayonets or Bowie knives.

The graves of these two Tigers were known to local citizens and kept untouched until 1979, when they were removed due to suburban development and reburied in the cemetery adjoining Saint John's Episcopal Church in Centreville.

7

Prince William County

The Potomac River Blockade

After its victory at First Manassas, the Confederate army established a defensive line from Centreville along the Occoquan River to the Potomac River. The Confederates used the banks of the Potomac as gun positions to halt Union traffic on the river, protecting Manassas Junction to the west and Fredericksburg to the south, and to close the Potomac River to shipping and isolate Washington City.

From May 29 until June 1, just below Prince William County in Stafford County, the Battle of Aquia Creek was the first exchange of cannon fire between Union navy gunboats and Confederate shore batteries in the Northern Virginia region. The Confederates set up several shore batteries to block Union military and commercial vessels from moving in from the Chesapeake Bay and along the lower Potomac, as well as for defensive purposes. The battery at Aquia also was intended to protect the railroad terminal at that location. The Union forces sought to destroy or remove these batteries as part of the effort to blockade Confederate coastal and Chesapeake Bay ports. The battle was tactically inconclusive. Each side inflicted little damage and no serious casualties on the other. The Union vessels were unable to dislodge the Confederates from their positions or to inflict serious casualties on their garrisons or serious damage to their batteries. The Confederates manning the batteries were unable to inflict serious casualties on the Union force or serious damage on their vessels.

On August 22, General Robert E. Lee issued orders to blockade the Potomac by building a series of artillery positions that would command the sailing channel. One of these positions was on the grounds of his ancestral home, Leesylvania, also known as Freestone Point. His father, "Light Horse Harry" Lee, was born there. By October, the Confederates had constructed batteries at Evansport (now downtown Quantico), consisting of two batteries on the river bank and another four hundred yards inland; a field battery located at the mouth of Chopawamsic Creek, where it empties into the Potomac (now the Marine Corps Air Facility); and Shipping Point (now Hospital Point on Quantico), number of guns unknown. Freestone Point became a four-gun battery on the shore of the Potomac (now within Leesylvania State Park), and Cockpit Point (near the current asphalt plant in Dumfries), consisting of six guns (one heavy gun) in four batteries, a powder magazine and rear rifle pits, on top of a seventy-five-foot-high cliff known as Possum Nose. By mid-December, the Confederates had thirty-seven heavy guns in position along the river.

On September 25, 1861, the Freestone Point batteries were shelled by the USS *Jacob Bell*, commanded by Lieutenant Edward P. McCrea, and the USS *Seminole*, commanded by Lieutenant Charles S. Norton. They fired on the point to disperse the workers and in turn were fired upon by the Confederates. The action lasted most of the afternoon, with little damage done by either side. Sergeant Walter Curry of the Washington Mounted Artillery of Hampton's Legion wrote in his diary that "as soon as the eleventh shot was fired, our Guns opened on the Lincolnite men of war which were floating majestically on the broad Potomac."

An article dealing with the blockade appeared in *Harper's Weekly* on November 2, 1861, under the title "The Closing of the Potomac":

> It is known that the rebels have some fifteen miles of batteries on the south shore of the Potomac, and that every vessel which tries to pass is fired upon. Hence general alarm is felt throughout the North at the "closing of the Potomac," and loyal citizens are asking each other what General McClellan will do for fodder.
>
> If General McClellan has been taken by surprise by the erection of hostile batteries on the Potomac, he is not the man the people take him for. At least six weeks ago, it was apparent that the rebels had the power to plant cannon on the Virginia bank of the river, in such positions as to seriously menace passing craft. If General McClellan be the far-sighted general we believe him to be, he was prepared for what has happened, and is provided with a remedy.
>
> But there is no reason why the erection of batteries on the Potomac should be regarded as closing that river. Balls and shells are unpleasant things to

Freestone earthworks, part of the Confederate fortifications that blockaded the Potomac River below Washington City.

come into contact with, no doubt. It is, however, the business of vessels of war to encounter them and their captains can no more complain of being under fire than private soldiers. With one or two exceptions, the rebel batteries are a mile from the channel. At this distance the most experienced gunners will not sink one craft in twenty. It will be time enough to consider the Potomac closed when every other craft which tries to pass the batteries is sure of being sunk or destroyed.

CONFEDERATE WINTER CAMPS—FIGHTING BOREDOM AND DISEASE

As the Confederates settled along their defensive lines in Prince William County, many units constructed log huts with clapboard roofs to sit out the Northern Virginia winter. Those located in the Neabsco Creek and Quantico Creek areas also manned the various forts blockading the Potomac.

What later in the winter became General John Bell Hood's Texas Brigade constructed its winter camp on what is now the Prince William County Government and Police Center near Dumfries. It was named Camp Wigfall, in honor of their commander, Brigadier General Louis T. Wigfall, who took up residence near his encamped troops in a tavern at Dumfries, during the winter of 1861–62. He would frequently call the men to arms at midnight, imagining a Federal invasion. His nervousness was blamed on his fondness for whiskey and hard cider. He appeared visibly drunk, on and off-duty, in the presence of his men on more than one occasion. He resigned his commission in February 1862 to take a seat in the Confederate Senate (he had been a U.S. senator before Texas seceded), and was replaced by General Hood, whose brigade became one of General Lee's most trusted later in the war.

When not on picket duty, the men cooked and cleaned camp. For entertainment, they played cards, foraged and visited brigade sutlers or friends and relatives at nearby camps. They also built the Lone Star Theater for the newly formed Hood's Minstrels, a group of actors, brass band and choir. The theater was popular and featured performances by banjoist Sam Sweeney and "The Bonnie Blue Flag" lyricist Harry McCarty.

Shanties constructed in Centreville, Virginia, for the winter of 1861–62. Similar dwellings were used near the Potomac batteries.

Unsanitary conditions and crowding in the camps contributed to outbreaks of measles, dysentery, diarrhea and typhoid fever, causing more deaths than by combat. Most soldiers, like the Texans, were from the Deep South and unused to the cold of Northern Virginia. They relied on local citizens for care, while the army doctors struggled to control the epidemics. Wrote Private James M. Polk, Fourth Texas Infantry, "Our losses in the winter of 1861 from sickness and exposure, incident to camp life, were very heavy. I had the measles; had a relapse and developed a case of typhoid-pneumonia, and my fate was uncertain for six weeks. For ten or twelve days I did not eat a mouthful of anything."

The nearby village of Dumfries, former Prince William County seat, became strategically significant to the winter camps set up nearby. General William H.C. Whiting had his headquarters at Love's Tavern, a prominent way station going back to the mid-1700s (now home of Prince William County's Historic Preservation Division). The most important event happened in November 1861, when the *Richmond Times Dispatch* reported that "General Johnston arrived here [Dumfries] this evening, and is now staying at Gen. Whiting's head quarters. He will remain here a day or two inspecting the army and then return to Centreville. His arrival has been a course of much rejoicing, and hundreds have been in town today, to get a glimpse of their Chief. They will have an opportunity tomorrow." By March 1862, the Confederate troops had moved out and Federal soldiers had arrived, keeping control for the rest of the war.

8

Loudoun County

The Battle of Ball's Bluff

Loudoun County, now part of Virginia's Horse and Wine Country, was destined to be an area of significant military activity during the war. Located on Virginia's northern frontier, with its Heights overlooking Harpers Ferry and bounded by the Potomac River on the east, Loudoun County became a borderland after Virginia's secession. The numerous Potomac bridges, ferries and fords made it an ideal location for Federal and Confederate armies to cross into and out of Virginia. Likewise, the county's several gaps in the Blue Ridge Mountains that connected the Piedmont to the Shenandoah Valley and Winchester were of considerable strategic importance. The opposing armies would traverse the county several times throughout the war, leading to several small battles, most notably the Battle of Ball's Bluff in October 1861.

The fertile Loudoun Valley, with its wealth of produce and livestock, was of vital importance to the Confederacy and ideal to provide forage for the Union army. Furthermore, the local population was deeply divided over secession, with tensions and hostilities against one-time neighbors added to the death and destruction wrought during the war. In the November 1860 election, the county had voted overwhelmingly for John Bell, the Constitutional Union candidate. Bitter partisan warfare kept hostilities active even when the armies where far from Loudoun County. It has been said that no county in Virginia that did not witness a decisive battle suffered more than Loudoun. The Loudoun Rangers have the distinction of being the only unit raised in present-day Virginia to serve in the Union army.

Loudoun served initially as an outpost of the Confederate army based out of Winchester. From the garrison at Leesburg, the Confederates conducted raids and recruitment drives into central Maryland, carting away men and supplies, as well as threatening the C&O Canal, the B&O Railroad and Washington City. To meet this threat, Federals deployed along the Loudoun-Maryland border, leading to many skirmishes at the strategic river crossings.

THE ROCKVILLE EXPEDITION AND THE FIRST LOUDOUNER KILLED IN THE COUNTY

The June 1861 Rockville Expedition, one of the first offensive movements by Union forces, was ordered by General Winfield Scott for the purpose of securing firmly in Union hands the area of Maryland along the Potomac River northwest of Washington. Scott wanted to cut off the flow of supplies from Baltimore to Virginia, protect the area from Rebel raids, reopen the obstructed C&O Canal and "give countenance to our friends in Maryland and Virginia."

Colonel Charles P. Stone was selected to lead the twenty-five-hundred-man Union force, which was composed of three regiments plus four battalions of infantry, two companies of mounted troops and two cannons. Stone's command departed from Washington on June 10 and arrived at Rockville, Maryland, the next day. Stone established his headquarters at Rockville and dispatched detachments to numerous nearby river towns. The sudden appearance of Union troops in the area alarmed Confederates in Virginia and Rebel sympathizers in Maryland. On June 14, one of Stone's detachments engaged in an inconsequential skirmish with local Confederates at the river town of Seneca Mills, Maryland. The next day, his men secured Edward's Ferry and Conrad's Ferry, the two main approaches to the strategic Loudoun town of Leesburg.

Confederate forces advanced to the river from Leesburg on the sixteenth, but Stone's artillery forced them to retreat the next day when they attempted to cross at Edward's Ferry. The Union force continued to occupy the area for the next two weeks. They then received new orders from Scott to march northwestward to Martinsburg (now West Virginia) and join forces with General Robert Patterson's command, which was arriving from Pennsylvania. When Stone's men reached Harpers Ferry, they found that the Confederate occupiers had evacuated the town. Stone crossed over the river and engaged in a long-range artillery duel with the Rebel rear guard. The Rockville Expedition ended on July 7, when the Union troops arrived in Martinsburg.

On August 5, 1861, Loudoun County lost its first citizen/soldier on Loudoun soil. Loudoun had already painted the hills and fertile farm soil along the banks of Bull Run Creek with the blood of its Confederate sons, but that was Prince William County, not Loudoun. On the evening of August 4, 1861, a raiding party of approximately fifty or sixty men of the First Independent New York Battery (which would become part of the Forty-eighth New York Infantry) crossed over the Potomac River at Berlin, Maryland (now

The cover of the sesquicentennial program for the remembrance of Cumberland George Orrison, first Loudoun Confederate killed in Loudoun County.

Brunswick). They were itching for action, having missed out at Manassas because of being attached to General Patterson's army. At approximately 7:00 p.m., they headed for Lovettsville, where they captured two Rebels. From Lovettsville, they headed eastward, somewhat following the old road that ran along the river. Arriving opposite Point of Rocks about daylight, they descended on and surprised a Rebel picket post of twenty-one men from the Loudoun Cavalry. After the smoke had cleared, six men of the Loudoun Cavalry had been captured, and one man, Private Cumberland George Orrison, lay dead on the ground.

THE BATTLE OF BALL'S BLUFF

The Battle of Ball's Bluff, also known as the Battle of Harrison's Island or the Battle of Leesburg, was fought on October 21, 1861, in Loudoun County as part of General McClellan's operations in Northern Virginia. While a minor engagement in comparison with the battles that would take place in years to follow, it was the second largest battle of the Eastern Theater in 1861 and, in its aftermath, had repercussions in the Union army's chain of command structure. It also raised separation of powers issues under the Constitution during the war.

In the weeks preceding the battle, McClellan had been promoted to general-in-chief of all Union armies, and now, three months after First Manassas, he was building up the Union Army of the Potomac in preparation for an eventual advance into Virginia. On October 19, McClellan ordered Brigadier General George A. McCall to march his division from his camp in Fairfax County to Dranesville, twelve miles southeast of Leesburg, in order to discover the purpose of recent Confederate troop movements that indicated that General Nathan Evans might have abandoned Leesburg. Evans had, in fact, left the town on October 16–17 but had done so on his own authority. When General Beauregard expressed his displeasure at this move, Evans returned. By the evening of October 19, he had taken up a defensive position on the Alexandria–Winchester Turnpike (modern-day Route 7) east of town.

McClellan came to Dranesville to consult with McCall that same evening and ordered McCall to return to his main camp at Langley the following morning. However, McCall requested additional time to complete some mapping of the roads in the area and, as a result, did not actually leave for Langley until the morning of October 21, just as the fighting at Ball's Bluff was heating up. On October 20, while McCall was completing his mapping, McClellan ordered Brigadier General Charles P. Stone to conduct what he called "a slight demonstration" in order to see how the Confederates might react. Stone moved troops to the river at Edward's Ferry, positioned other forces along the river, had his artillery fire into suspected Confederate positions and briefly crossed about one hundred men of the First Minnesota to the Virginia shore just before dusk. Having gotten no reaction from Evans with all of this activity, Stone recalled his troops to their camps, and the "slight demonstration" came to an end.

Stone then ordered Colonel Charles Devens of the Fifteenth Massachusetts Infantry (stationed on Harrison's Island facing Ball's Bluff) to send a patrol across the river at that point to gather what information it could about enemy deployments. Devens sent Captain Chase Philbrick and approximately twenty men to carry out Stone's order. Advancing in the dark nearly a mile inland from the bluff, the inexperienced Philbrick mistook a row of trees or haystacks for the tents of a Confederate camp and, without verifying what he saw, returned and reported the existence of

Map of Ball's Bluff, considered the worst Union disaster after First Manassas.

a camp. Stone immediately ordered Devens to cross some three hundred men and, as soon as it was light enough to see, attack the camp and, per his orders, "return to your present position."

This was the genesis of the Battle of Ball's Bluff. Contrary to the long-held traditional interpretation, it did not come from a plan by either McClellan or Stone to take Leesburg. The initial crossing of troops was meant as a small reconnaissance. That was followed by what was intended to be a raiding party. On the morning of October 21, Colonel Devens's raiding party discovered the mistake made the previous evening by the patrol; there was no camp to raid. Opting not to recross the river immediately, Devens deployed his men in a tree line and sent a messenger back to report to Stone and get new instructions. On hearing the messenger's report, Stone sent him back to tell Devens that the remainder of the Fifteenth Massachusetts (another 350 men) would cross the river and move to his position. When they arrived, Devens was to turn his raiding party back into a reconnaissance and move toward Leesburg.

While the messenger was going back to Colonel Devens with this new information, Colonel (and U.S. senator) Edward D. Baker showed up at Stone's camp to find out about the morning's events. Baker and Abraham Lincoln had been friends since the 1830s. Baker had gone to California in the early 1850s and by the end of 1860 was one of the first senators from Oregon. In May 1861, Senator Baker had been authorized by the secretary of war to organize an infantry regiment to be taken as part of the quota from California. Recruiting mostly in Philadelphia, Baker raised the California Brigade and served as its colonel. A few months later, he was assigned command of a brigade guarding the fords along the Potomac River. He had been offered a generalship but would have had to quit the Senate to accept it. Baker had not been involved in any of the activities to that point. Stone told him of the mistake about the camp and about his new orders to reinforce Devens for reconnaissance purposes. He then instructed Baker to go to the crossing point, evaluate the situation and either withdraw the troops already in Virginia or cross additional troops at his discretion.

On the way upriver to execute this order, Baker met Devens's messenger coming back a second time to report that Devens and his men had encountered and briefly engaged the enemy, one company (Company K) of the Seventeenth Mississippi Infantry. Baker immediately ordered as many troops as he could find to cross the river, but he did so without determining what boats were available to do this. A bottleneck quickly developed so that Union troops could only cross slowly and in small numbers, making the crossing last throughout the day.

Meanwhile, Devens's men (now about 650 strong) remained in its advanced position and engaged in two additional skirmishes with a growing force of Confederates, while other Union troops crossed the river but deployed near the bluff and did not advance from there. Devens finally withdrew at about 2:00 p.m. and met Baker, who had finally crossed the river half an hour earlier. Beginning at about 3:00 p.m., the fighting began in earnest and was almost continuous until just after dark.

Colonel Baker was killed at about 4:30 p.m. and remains the only U.S. senator ever killed in battle. Following an abortive attempt to break out of their constricted position around the bluff, the Federals began to recross the river in some disarray. Shortly before dark, a fresh Confederate regiment (the remainder of the Seventeenth Mississippi) arrived and formed the core of the climactic assault that finally broke and routed the Union troops.

Many of the Union soldiers were driven down the steep slope at the southern end of Ball's Bluff (behind the current location of the national cemetery) and into the river. Boats attempting to cross back to Harrison Island were soon swamped and capsized. Many Federals, including some of the wounded, were drowned. Bodies floated downriver to Washington City and even as far as Mount Vernon in the days following the battle. A total of 223 Federals were killed, 226 were wounded and 553 were captured on the banks of the Potomac later that night. The *Official Records* incorrectly states that only 49 Federals were killed at this battle, an error probably resulting from a mistaken reading of the report of the Union burial detail that crossed over the next day under a flag of truce. Fifty-four Union dead—of whom only 1 is identified—are buried in Ball's Bluff Battlefield and National Cemetery.

This Union defeat was relatively minor in comparison to the battles to come in the war, but it had a wide impact in and out of military affairs. Due to the loss of a sitting senator, it led to severe political ramifications in

A lithograph of the Battle of Ball's Bluff shows Union troops rushing into the Potomac River, being pursued by Confederate forces. *Courtesy of Douglas Bostick.*

Washington City. General Stone was treated as the scapegoat for the defeat, but members of Congress suspected that there was a conspiracy to betray the Union. The ensuing outcry, and a desire to learn why Federal forces had lost battles at Manassas (Bull Run), Wilson's Creek (in August in Missouri, called the "Bull Run of the West") and Ball's Bluff, led to the establishment of the Congressional Joint Committee on the Conduct of the War, which would bedevil Union officers for the remainder of the war (particularly those who were Democrats) and contribute to nasty political infighting among the generals in the high command.

Composed of three senators and four representatives, this committee remained in session throughout the war and gave itself the power to investigate anything or anyone. Its first investigation dealt with Ball's Bluff. Its first victim was General Stone. Going after Stone more for political reasons than because he had lost a battle, the committee allowed hearsay and complaints by officers whom General Stone had previously disciplined to count as valid testimony. The sessions were closed, and Stone himself was questioned without being informed that he had become the target of the investigation. Stone was arrested in front of his Washington home near midnight on February 8, 1862.

Stone was imprisoned in New York at Forts Lafayette and Hamilton for six months with no charges ever being filed against him. He finally was released on August 16, 1862.

Lieutenant Oliver Wendell Holmes Jr., of the Twentieth Massachusetts Volunteer Infantry, survived a nearly fatal wound at Ball's Bluff to become an associate justice of the Supreme Court forty years later. During 1861, Holmes had written a new verse for "The Star Spangled Banner":

> *When our land is illumined with liberty's smile,*
> *If a foe from within strikes a blow at her glory,*
> *Down, down with the traitor that tries to defile*
> *The flag of the stars, and the page of her story!*
> *By the millions unchained,*
> *Who their birthright have gained*
> *We will keep her bright blazon forever unstained;*
> *And the star-spangled banner in triumph shall wave,*
> *While the land of the free is the home of the brave.*

Herman Melville's poem "Ball's Bluff—A Reverie" (published in 1866) commemorates the battle. Holmes's great friend and role model Lieutenant

Henry Livermore Abbot also survived the battle but did not survive the war. In 1865, Abbott was posthumously promoted to brigadier general. Another outstanding young officer named Edmund Rice also eventually reached the rank of brigadier general, was awarded the Congressional Medal of Honor and was fortunate enough to survive the war by near a half century. John William Grout was killed in the battle; his death inspired a poem (and later a song) titled "The Vacant Chair."

The site of the battle is being restored today, with ongoing efforts by volunteers thinning out the overgrowth and making interpretation of the battlefield much easier. A sesquicentennial reenactment of the battle was held on the actual battlefield on October 22, 2011. But the area near the Bluff and Potomac River still appears as wild as it did in that October 1861. It is preserved as the Ball's Bluff Battlefield and National Cemetery, which was declared a National Historic Landmark in 1984. The park is maintained by the Northern Virginia Regional Park Authority.

I include here the official reports from the commanders of the Thirteenth Mississippi (CSA) and Fifteenth Massachusetts (USA).

THE BATTLE OF BALL'S BLUFF

Report of Col. William Barksdale, Thirteenth Mississippi Infantry.

REGIMENTAL HEADQUARTERS,
Fort Evans, near Leesburg, October 28, 1861.
General N.G. Evans,
Headquarters, Leesburg.

GENERAL: I have the honor to report that in obedience to your orders I left my encampment near Ball's Mill, on Goose Creek, with my regiment, on Sunday morning, the 20th instant, at 5 o'clock, and encamped the following night on the Alexandria turnpike road, near the Burnt Bridge over Goose Creek, about 4 miles east from Leesburg, with the Eighth Virginia Regiment, Colonel Hunton, on my right, and the Seventeenth Mississippi Regiment, Colonel Featherston, on my left.

Early on Monday morning the guns of the enemy opened upon us from their batteries on the Maryland side of the Potomac River, but without effect. At 8 o'clock I proceeded with my regiment to Fort Evans, and forthwith took position in the woods to the right of the fort, where I could observe the movements of the enemy.

About 12 o'clock I dispatched Capt. L.D. Fletcher's company (D) to report to you at Fort Evans. I herewith inclose his report of the company's movements that day. During the whole of the engagement it was in the thickest of the fight, rendering efficient service, and bearing itself with undaunted courage.

About 1.30 o'clock I was ordered by you to advance in the direction of Edward's Ferry, and to ascertain the position and number of the enemy. I marched at once in that direction, and halted in a skirt of woods near the Daily house, at the same time directing Captain McIntosh to skirmish in the woods and near the river on the left, and Captain Eckford, with a platoon of his company, to skirmish on the right of that house, and report without delay the result of their observation. Both reported that the enemy was in force in large numbers on this side of the river and just beyond the Daily house. I immediately ordered the regiment to advance, and when near the house a number of shots were fired by the advance guard on both sides, killing one man of my regiment. The loss of the enemy not ascertained.

Perceiving that the object of the enemy was to outflank me on the right, and learning that Colonels Burt and Featherston, with their respective commands, had been ordered in another direction, I formed my regiment on the right of the Edward's Ferry road, intending to commence the attack from the woods stretching alongside Daily plantation and to the right of the house, at the same time directing Captain Bradley to skirmish on the left and Captain Worthington on the right.

At this moment I was ordered by you to hasten to the support of the Eighth Virginia Regiment and the Seventeenth and Eighteenth Mississippi Regiments, which were engaged with the enemy 2 miles from Edward's Ferry and near Conrad's Ferry. I at once, and in double-quick time, started to their relief, leaving Captain Worthington's company to observe the movements of the enemy at Edward's Ferry, but before reaching the scene of action I received two peremptory orders from you to return to the vicinity of Fort Evans, which was accordingly done, directing the companies of Captains Randell, McIntosh, and Worthington to remain in the rear, to prevent the advance of the enemy that night from Edward's Ferry.

I am satisfied that the presence of my command in position at Edward's Ferry prevented the advance of a large column of the enemy, which was intended to re-enforce General Baker's command near Conrad's Ferry, then engaged in battle with our forces.

On Tuesday morning I was ordered by you to reconnoiter the enemy at Edward's Ferry, and attack him if in my judgment his numbers and position would warrant me in doing so. Reaching the ground I occupied the day before, I ordered Captain Randell to skirmish on my left and Captain Eckford on my right. They reported that the enemy in very large numbers was stationed, as on the preceding day, near the banks of the river. From their movements, which could be easily seen from my position, I supposed they were planting a battery at the

Confederate general Nathan "Shanks" Evans, Rebel commander at Ball's Bluff.

point of woods jutting out into the field to the right of the Daily house. I determined to make the attack at that point, and accordingly ordered Captain Eckford to advance with his and Captain McElroy's companies, to commence the engagement, and to charge and take the battery, if one should be found there.

Taking the road leading to Kephart's Mill, I halted the regiment in the woods to the right of the Daily plantation, and in a few minutes Captain Eckford commenced the attack upon several companies of pickets which were stationed along the field; charging upon and driving them in great disorder and confusion before his fire. I ordered the regiment at once to advance, and the engagement in a moment became general. Under a heavy fire from the enemy's batteries on both sides of the river and an incessant fire from his lines on this side the regiment continued to advance some 400 yards, firing as it advanced, driving the enemy before it back to the river, and killing, so far as I have been able to learn, 35 or 40 of their number. The enemy having been driven back behind his field works, and greatly outnumbering my command, having also artillery on both sides of the river, I did not deem it proper further to continue the assault, and hence withdrew the regiment to its position near Fort Evans, which I reached some time after dark. I herewith inclose Captain Eckford's report.

Every order I gave during both days was obeyed with promptness and alacrity, and the engagement on Tuesday was marked by the greatest possible zeal, courage, and enthusiasm on the part of both officers and men.

WILLIAM BARKSDALE,
Colonel, Comdg. Thirteenth Regiment Mississippi Volunteers.

THE BATTLE OF BALL'S BLUFF

Report of Col. Charles Devens, Fifteenth Massachusetts Infantry

HDQRS. FIFTEENTH REGIMENT MASS. VOLUNTEERS,
Poolesville, Md., October 23, 1861.

GENERAL: *I respectfully report that about 12 o'clock Sunday night, October 20, I crossed the Potomac by your order from Harrison's Island to the Virginia shore with five companies, numbering about 300 men, of my regiment, with the intention of taking a rebel camp, reported by scouts to be situated at the distance of about a mile from the river, of destroying the same, of observing the country around, and of returning to the river, or of waiting and reporting if I thought myself able to remain for re-enforcements, or if I found a position capable of being defended against a largely superior force. Having only three boats, which together conveyed about 30 men; it was nearly 4 o'clock when all the force was transferred to the opposite shore. We passed down the river about 60 rods by a path discovered by the scouts, and then up the bluff known as Ball's Bluff, where we found an open field surrounded by woods. At this point we halted until daybreak, being joined here by a company of 100 men from the Twentieth Massachusetts, accompanied by Colonel Lee, who were to protect our return.*

At daybreak we pushed forward our reconnaissance towards Leesburg to the distance of about a mile from the river, to a spot supposed to be the site of the rebel encampment, but found on passing through the woods that the scouts had been deceived by a line of trees on the brow of the slope, the opening through which presented, in an uncertain light, somewhat the appearance of a line of tents. Leaving the detachment in the woods, I proceeded with Captain Philbrick and two or three scouts across the slope and along the other line of it, observing Leesburg, which was in full view, and the country about it, as carefully as possible, and seeing but four tents of the enemy. My force being well concealed by the woods, and having no reason to believe my presence was discovered, and no large number of the enemy's tents being in sight, I determined not to return at once, but to report to yourself, which I did, by directing Quartermaster Howe to repair at once to Edward's Ferry to state these facts and to say that in my opinion I could remain until I was re-enforced.

The means of transportation between the island and the Virginia shore had been strengthened, I knew, at daybreak, by a large boat, which would convey 60 or 70 men at once, and as the boat could cross and recross every ten minutes, I had no reason to suppose there would be any difficulty in sending over 500 men in an hour, as it was known there were two large boats between the island and the Maryland shore, which would convey to the island all the troops that could be conveyed from it to the Virginia shore.

Mr. Howe left me with his instructions at about 6.30 a.m., and during his absence, at about 7 o'clock, a company of riflemen, who had probably discovered us, were reported on our right upon the road from Conrad's Ferry. I directed Captain Philbrick, Company H, to pass up over the slope and attack them, while Captain Rockwood, Company A, was ordered to proceed to the right and cut off their retreat in the direction of Conrad's Ferry, and accompany Captain Philbrick as he proceeded to execute the order. Captain Philbrick's command proceeded over the slope of the hill, and the enemy retreated down on the other side, taking the direction of a corn field in which the corn had lately been cut and stood in the shocks. The first volley was fired by them from a ditch or trench, into which they retreated. It was immediately returned by our men, and the skirmish continued hotly for some minutes. I had ordered Captain Forehand, Company G, to re-enforce Captain Philbrick, but a body of rebel cavalry being reported on our left, I directed Captain Philbrick to return to the wood, lest he might be cut off from the main body of the detachment. This he did in good order.

In the skirmish 9 men of Company H were wounded, 1 killed, and 2 were missing at its close, although the field was carefully examined by Captain Philbrick and myself before we left it. They probably were wounded and crawled into the bush, which was growing in portions of it.

On returning to the wood I remained waiting for an attack for perhaps half an hour. At the end of this time, as my messenger did not return, I deemed it prudent to join Colonel Lee, which I did; but after remaining with him upon the bluff a short time, and having thoroughly scouted the woods, I returned to my first position.

I was rejoined at 8 a.m. by Quartermaster Howe, who reported to me that I was to remain where I was, and would be re-enforced, and that Lieutenant-Colonel Ward would proceed to Smart's Mill with the remainder of the regiment, that a communication should be kept up between us, and that 10 cavalry would report to me for the purpose of reconnoitering. For some reason they never appeared or reported to me, but I have since learned they came as far as the bluff. If they had reported to me, they could have rendered excellent service. I directed Quartermaster Howe to return at once and report the skirmish that had taken place, and threw out a company of skirmishers to the brow of the hill, and also to my right and left, to await the arrival of more troops.

At about 10 o'clock Quartermaster Howe returned and stated that he had reported the skirmish of the morning, and that Colonel Baker would shortly arrive with his brigade and take command. Between 9 and 11 o'clock I was joined by Lieutenant-Colonel Ward with the remainder of my regiment, making, in all, a force of 625 men, with 28 officers, from my regiment, as reported to me by the adjutant, many of the men of the regiment being at this time on other duty.

About 12 o'clock it was reported to me a force was gathering on my left, and about 12.30 o'clock a strong attack was made on my left by a body of infantry concealed in the woods and upon the skirmishers in front by a body of cavalry. The fire of the enemy was resolutely returned by the regiment, which maintained its ground with entire determination. Re-enforcements not yet having arrived, and the attempts of the enemy to outflank us being vigorous, I directed the regiment to retire about 60 paces into an open space in the wood, and prepare to receive any attack that might be made, while I called in my skirmishers. When this was done I returned to the bluff, where Colonel Baker had already arrived. This was at 2.15 p.m. He directed me to form my regiment at the right of the position he proposed to occupy, which was done by eight companies, the center and left being composed of a detachment of the Twentieth Massachusetts, numbering about 300 men, under command of Colonel Lee. A battalion of the California regiment, numbering about 600 men, Lieutenant-Colonel Wistar commanding; 2 howitzers, commanded by Lieutenant French, and a 6-pounder, commanded by Lieutenant Bramhall, were planted in front, supported by Company D, Captain Studley, and Company F, Captain Sloan, of the Fifteenth Massachusetts.

The enemy soon appeared in force, and, after sharp skirmishing on the right, directed his attack upon our whole line, but more particularly upon our center and left, where it was gallantly met by the Twentieth Massachusetts and the California battalion. Skirmishing during all the action was very severe on the right, but the skirmishers of the enemy were resolutely repulsed by our own, composed of Companies A and I, Captains Rockwood and Joslin, of the Fifteenth Massachusetts, and Company --, of the Twentieth Massachusetts, under the direction of Major Kimball, of the Fifteenth Massachusetts.

General Charles P. Stone, Union commander at Ball's Bluff. His expansion of General McClellan's order to "cause a slight demonstration" led to Stone's arrest, the ruining of his military career and the establishment of a joint Senate-House War Oversight Committee.

The action commenced about 3 p.m., and at about 4 p.m. I was ordered to detach two companies from the left of my regiment to the support of the left of the line, and to draw in proportionately the right flank, which was done, Companies G and H, Captains Forehand and Philbrick, being detached for that purpose. By this time it had become painfully evident, by the volume and rapidity of the enemy's fire and the persistency of his attacks that he was in much larger force than we. The two howitzers were silent and the 6-pounder also. Their commander came from the field wounded.

Soon after I was called from the right of my regiment, there being at this time a comparative cessation of the enemy's fire, to the center of the line, and learned for the first time that Colonel Baker had been killed, and that Lieutenant-Colonel Ward, of the Fifteenth Massachusetts, had been carried from the field severely wounded. Colonel Lee supposing it his duty to take command, I reported myself ready to execute his orders. He expressed his opinion that the only thing to be done was to retreat to the river, and that the battle was utterly lost. It soon appeared that Colonel Cogswell was entitled to the command, which expressed his determination to make the attempt to cut our way to Edward's Ferry, and ordered me, as a preliminary movement, to form the Fifteenth Regiment in line towards the left. The Fifteenth Regiment accordingly moved across from the right to the left of the original line. Two or three companies of the Tammany New York regiment, just then arrived, formed also on its left. While endeavoring to make the necessary disposition to retreat, confusion was created by the appearance of an officer of the enemy's force in front of the Tammany regiment, who called on them to charge on the enemy, who were now in strong force along the wood occupied formerly by the Fifteenth Massachusetts during the former portion of the action. The detachment of the Tammany regiment, probably mistaking this for an order from their own officers, rushed forward to the charge, and the Fifteenth Massachusetts, supposing that an order had been given for the advance of the whole line, rushed with eagerness, but was promptly recalled by their officers, who had received no such order. The detachment of the regiment was received with a shower of bullets, and suffered severely. In the disturbance caused by their repulse the line was broken, but was promptly reformed.

After this, however, although several volleys were given and returned and the troops fought vigorously, it seemed impossible to preserve the order necessary for a combined military movement, and Colonel Cogswell reluctantly gave the order to retreat to the river bank. The troops descended the bluff, and reached the bank of the river where there is a narrow plateau between the river and the ascent of the bluff, both the plateau and the bluff being heavily wooded. As I descended upon this plateau, in company with Colonel Cogswell, I saw the large boat, upon which we depended as the means of crossing the river, swamped by the number of men who rushed upon it.

For the purpose of retarding as much as possible the approach of the enemy, by direction of Colonel Cogswell I ordered the Fifteenth Regiment to deploy as skirmishers over the bank of the river, which order was executed, and several volleys were given and returned between them and others of our forces and the enemy, who were now pressing upon us in great numbers and forcing down furious volleys on this plateau and into the river to prevent any escape. It was impossible longer to continue to resist, and I should have had no doubt, if we had been contending with the troops of a foreign nation, in justice to the lives of men, it would have been our duty to surrender; but it was impossible to do this to rebels and traitors, and I had no hesitation in advising men to escape as they could, ordering them in all cases to throw *their arms into the river rather than give them up to the enemy. This order was generally obeyed, although several of the men swam the river with their muskets on their backs, and others have returned to camp, bringing with them their muskets, who had remained on the Virginia shore for two nights rather than to part with their weapons in order to facilitate their escape.*

Having passed up along the line of that portion of the river occupied by my regiment, I returned to the lower end of it, and at dark myself swam the river by the aid of three of the soldiers of my regiment. On arriving at the island I immediately gathered a force of 30 men, who had reached it with safety, and placed them at the passage of the river to prevent any attempt of the enemy crossing in pursuit, but soon learned that Colonel Hinks had arrived with the Nineteenth Massachusetts Regiment, and would take charge of the island.

Our loss, in proportion to the numbers engaged of the regiment, is large, as will be seen by the list of the killed, missing, and wounded, which I annex. A large proportion of those reported missing are probably prisoners in the hands of the enemy.

Although the result of the day was most unfortunate, it is but justice to the officers and men of the Fifteenth Massachusetts Regiment, as well as to the other troops engaged, to say that they behaved most nobly during the entire day, and that the nation has no occasion to blush for dishonor to its arms. The loss of the regiment in arrest equipments, and clothing is necessarily heavy, the particulars of which I will immediately forward.

In conclusion, it may not be improper for me to say that, notwithstanding the regiment mourns the loss of the brave officers and soldiers whose names are borne on the list I annex, its spirit is entirely unbroken and its organization is in no way demoralized. It will answer any summons from you to another contest with the foe, although with diminished numbers, with as hearty a zest as on the morning of October 21.

I remain, general, respectfully,
CHAS. DEVENS,
Colonel.

A hero on the Confederate side was Elijah V. White. "One of the best cavalry officers we have," said Confederate general A.P. Hill about White, who later became colonel and commander of a cavalry battalion known as

The cemetery on the Ball's Bluff battlefield is one of the smallest national cemeteries in the United States. Fifty-four Union army dead from the battle are interred in twenty-five graves in the half-acre plot; the identities of all of the interred—except for one, James Allen of the Fifteenth Massachusetts—are unknown.

the Commanches. Born in Poolesville, Maryland, White was a well-educated farmer in Loudoun County at the start of the war. His military experience included the Missouri border fighting of the 1850s and as a corporal in a local militia company, the Loudoun Cavalry. When his militia unit was transferred to the Confederacy, White began his war career as a private in Turner Ashby's Seventh Virginia Cavalry Regiment.

In October 1861, White was at home on leave and riding in a buggy with a lady friend when he heard the opening shots of the battle; he rushed to the scene to join the fight. He volunteered his services to General Evans and acted as a courier, scout and "all-purpose" soldier. Elijah was instrumental in the capture of over three hundred Union troops trapped below the bluffs. He was even mentioned by name in the after-action reports of three regiments: the Seventeenth Mississippi Infantry, the Eighth Virginia Infantry and this one from Jenifer's Cavalry:

Mr. White, of Colonel Ashby's cavalry, volunteered his services during the day. I never witnessed more coolness and courage than the young man displayed, being exposed to the heaviest fire of the enemy. He rode in front of a part of the Seventeenth Mississippi, ordering and encouraging the men.

Soon afterward, Elijah accepted a captaincy in the Confederate army and worked to raise a small company of couriers between Leesburg and Winchester. After the war, he purchased Conrad's Ferry, making many improvements and updating the cable ferryboat, renaming it the *General Jubal A. Early* after his former Confederate commander. Now renamed White's Ferry, it remains the only ferry still in use on the Potomac River.

9

The Battle of Dranesville

Border of Fairfax/Loudoun Counties

D ranesville, still a small village, is located about twenty miles northwest from Washington and about fourteen miles southeast from Leesburg. The road, connecting Dranesville and Leesburg, was a main line of travel and commerce until it was supplanted by the railroad, now supplanted by Virginia Route 7. Long caravans of Conestoga wagons with white canvas tops; droves of horses, sheep and cattle; and stagecoaches loaded with passengers gave life to the old road and brought prosperity to the surrounding area. The early nineteenth century was the golden age of the wagon road and tavern. With the coming of the railroad, wagons, stagecoaches and taverns were relegated to that long-gone era. The jangling of the wagon bells, the tooting of the stage-drivers' horns, the noisy commotion of the wayside inn are now forgotten echoes. Progress has her victims no less than war.

Dranesville was a recipient of the bounty that flowed from the old-time commerce. With the passing of the turnpike traffic, an unbroken quiet settled upon the village until the stillness was rudely broken on a memorable winter afternoon in 1861. The roar of cannons and the rattle of musketry announced to the village and the surrounding country that the tide of war, which had rolled at a distance, was now right at hand.

COMPARATIVE ESTIMATES

Compared with other engagements, this so-called Battle of Dranesville is but an insignificant incident in the War Between the States. Measured by the slaughter of such conflicts as First Manassas or Antietam, it assumes little more than the dimensions of a hotly contested skirmish. Yet in that first year of the war, it was called a battle, and to it, at the time, there was attached an importance that today is scarcely justified.

The Northern press proudly pointed to it as "the first Federal victory south of the Potomac." Secretary of War Cameron wrote to General McCall a few days after the battle:

> *It is one of the bright spots that give assurance of the success of coming events, and its effects must be to inspire confidence in the belief that hereafter, as heretofore, the cause of our country will triumph…Other portions of the army will be stimulated by their brave deeds, and men will be proud to say that at Dranesville they served under McCall and Ord.*

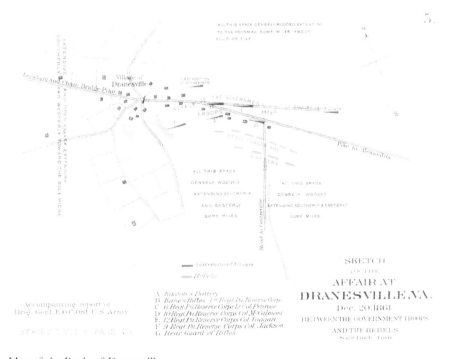

Map of the Battle of Dranesville.

Small was the victory, yet the semblance of success went far toward relieving the gloom of the disastrous rout at Manassas and the bloody repulse at Ball's Bluff. The collision of five regiments of Federals with four of Confederates on December 20, 1861, constitutes this battle. That first Christmas of the war was approaching, and the joyous memories of this happy festival emphasized the sorrow in countless homes, both North and South, where anxious hearts awaited its coming oppressed by the lengthening shadow of the great national tragedy that had already begun. Two deadly engagements had claimed their victims, and many a home was desolate.

The Federal army, disorganized and routed at Manassas, had retreated to the defenses of Washington. A line, stretching from the Chain Bridge to Alexandria along the south bank of the Potomac, formed a bulwark of forts between the capital and the victorious Confederates encamped at Centreville, some thirty miles away. McClellan had spent the summer and autumn in the task of transforming a uniformed mob of citizens into a well-disciplined army of soldiers. The guns of Manassas had quieted the clamorous cry of "On to Richmond," and the North was awaking to the fact that the road to the Confederate capital, if traveled at all, must be traveled by a well-trained army and was not to be attempted by a motley mob.

The Federal right, encamped at Langley, a few miles in advance of the Chain Bridge (three miles above Washington), consisted of the First Pennsylvania Reserves, commanded by Brigadier General George A. McCall, a West Pointer, who had seen active service in the Mexican War. The Reserves were formed in three brigades and commanded by generals who would earn distinction later in the war: the First, by Brigadier General John F. Reynolds; the Second, by Brigadier General George G. Meade; and the Third, by Brigadier General E.O.C. Ord. The Confederates were wintering at Centreville a few miles in advance of the line of Bull Run.

THE ARMY SPIRIT

The spirit pervading the two armies at this time afforded a striking contrast. The Federal army, beaten disastrously at Bull Run and completely discomfited in October at Ball's Bluff, had no precedents of victory to inspire it as a military organization. However great the bravery of the individual soldier may have been, the lack of confidence in the army as a fighting machine had assumed an all-pervasive form of panicked timidity. The Battle of Dranesville did timely service in removing, to a degree, this feeling of distrust.

Inspired by two signal victories, the Confederates were in fine form. The men in gray had gone to the front possessed with the idea that the South could "whip the world." Manassas and Ball's Bluff were but anticipated confirmations of this bold confidence. The successful issue of these initial combats beckoned to greater glories and the final triumph of the newly established Confederacy. This feeling animated the entire Confederate camp, and the army of Joe Johnston stood boldly and confidently awaiting the first hostile move of McClellan.

This was the environment when the Battle of Dranesville was fought. The tedium of winter quarters was relieved in both camps by sending out foraging parties, which also gathered information on the enemy. The arena of these sporadic operations was that portion of Fairfax County lying between Washington and Centreville. This strip of territory for months was no man's land—a region where terrifying rumors and dire alarms were continually afloat.

The citizens whose homes stood between the lines of the two opposing armies were divided in political sentiment. A few remained Union to the core, while the greater majority were heart and soul with the Confederacy. This division of sentiment filled the days and nights with a turmoil of excitement. Credence was given to the most improbable rumors, and accurate information was at a decided discount. A serious report reached McCall at Camp Pierpoint (Langley, the right of the Federal line) that a considerable body of Confederate cavalry was between Dranesville and the Potomac, menacing the Federal picket line and harassing Union citizens residing in that locality. In fact, it was known that two Unionist citizens had been arrested and had been sent on to Richmond to enjoy the hospitality of Libby Prison. Stirred by this rumor, on December 19, McCall issued an order to General Ord, commander of the Third Brigade of Pennsylvania Reserves (Sixth, Ninth, Tenth and Twelfth Regiments), to proceed the next morning at 6:00 a.m. with his brigade on the Leesburg Pike in the direction of Dranesville. Kane's famous "Bucktail" Regiment; Easton's Battery A, First Pennsylvania Artillery; and two squadrons of the First Pennsylvania Cavalry were directed to accompany this expedition.

The object of this demonstration, as indicated in McCall's order, was twofold: "to drive back the enemy's pickets from their advanced position" and to "procure a supply of forage." The latter was to be procured, according to the orders of the day, "at Gunnell's or any other rank secessionist in the neighborhood." The band of marauders between Dranesville and the river was not to be neglected.

MOVEMENTS OF THE TROOPS

The First Brigade, commanded by General Reynolds, was ordered to move to Difficult Run, a small stream that crossed the road between Dranesville and Langley, so as to be in supporting distance should Ord need assistance. It is humorous that in McCall's serious caution to Ord, he is ordered to bring his troops back to camp before nightfall without fail. It was evidently considered dangerous at this period to leave small bodies of troops out overnight.

Following orders, the expedition started at 6:00 a.m. on December 20. The day was cold, bright and clear. On the march, Ord learned that the Confederate marauders had decamped but that there was a respectable picket at Dranesville, which might be captured. Moving forward cautiously, he entered Dranesville about midday. He was accompanied by his cavalry and artillery, the infantry moving up at some distance in the rear. Upon Ord's approach, the Confederate cavalry picket stationed in the village fled and scattered but remained in the distance, watching the movements of the Federals.

Ord placed two guns of Easton's Battery on the hill near the church. From this vantage point, he scanned the open country lying before him in the direction of Leesburg. The scurrying of the Confederate pickets along a road in the distance and their

Confederate cavalry general J.E.B. Stuart. His foraging raid ran into a similar Union advance, which resulted in the Battle of Dranesville.

return for observation convinced him that a considerable body of the enemy was near at hand. He was not mistaken in this conjecture. General Johnston had sent out from his camp at Centreville nearly all the wagons of his army into upper Fairfax and lower Loudoun to gather much-needed supplies. The protection of this wagon train was entrusted to General J.E.B. Stuart. As a guard for the wagons, he had under his command four regiments of infantry (the Tenth Alabama, Sixth South Carolina, Eleventh Virginia and First Kentucky) one battery of four guns, the Sumter Flying Artillery of Georgia, and about 150 cavalry.

The two combatants, thus unexpectedly facing each other, were both seized with consternation. Ord came to the conclusion that the Confederate force in his front had been sent out to intercept his retreat to camp and capture his command. Stuart, on the other hand, could only interpret the presence of such a large body of the enemy as an attempt of the Federals to capture his wagons and forage.

He fully realized the danger of his position, as his wagons were scattered about the country gathering hay and corn, while the enemy could easily interpose between him and Johnston's camp at Centreville. Thus, both commanders, misconceiving the purpose of the other, immediately took steps to avert the imagined danger. These precautionary measures brought on the collision that is dignified by the name of the Battle of Dranesville. After the battle, both sides laid claim to the victory. This is now easily understood, for Ord felt that the battle had saved his command, and Stuart felt that it had saved all the wagons of Johnston's army and a valuable amount of supplies. Each accomplished what he conceived to be the main purpose of the battle, which, after all, was a misconception on the part of both, as Ord was not in pursuit of Stuart's wagon train and Stuart had no designs against Ord's line of retreat.

Ord's Artillery

Ord, in entering the village and placing a section of his artillery on the church hill, had passed the junction of the two roads on the higher hill some six hundred yards in his rear. This place, known as Drane Hill, is the military key of the situation, as it commands all of the surrounding country. Stuart knew this and immediately started to gain it by a circuitous march through the woods around Ord's flank. Stuart afterward stated that,

General Edward O.C. Ord, Union commander at Dranesville. This December 20 Federal victory helped end 1861 on a relatively high note for the Union.

had he gained this point with his four regiments, he could have held the whole Federal army in check.

Ord surmised, correctly, that the Confederates were moving around to his rear in the hope of seizing this coveted position. He immediately ordered the section of artillery that had taken its position near the church to withdraw and, with the other guns of the battery, to take position on Drane Hill, near the junction. This was done with commendable speed; the guns went at a sweeping gallop to the top of the hill and took a new position with muzzles pointing south. In this direction, the advance of the Confederates was driving in the Federal skirmish line. The Centreville Road entered the Alexandria Pike a short distance from the junction of that road with the Washington Pike.

The Confederate advance was along this Centreville Road, and Easton's Battery arrived in the nick of time to cover this important approach. Ord's foresight and promptness had secured for his troops an overmastering superiority of position. The Confederates, owing to the length and many difficulties of their circuitous march, had failed to reach the crest of the hill in advance of the Federals. Finding the enemy in secure possession of the coveted position, Stuart placed his battery in the Centreville Road some five or six hundred yards distant from the Federal artillery. This battery was placed behind a slight swell of ground, the muzzles of the guns just clearing this slight elevation. It came into action at once and poured a heavy fire into the ranks of the Federals, but this fire did little damage, being aimed too high.

Captain Easton, in command of the Federal battery, had no other target than the rising smoke, yet training his guns on the point where he thought the opposing battery ought to be, at the third fire he completely disabled the enemy's guns. One gun was put out of action, a caisson was exploded and many men and horses of the battery were killed, while many more were dangerously wounded. General Stuart, in his report of the battle, wrote, "Every shot of the enemy was dealing destruction on man, limber and horse."

The two batteries thus engaged marked the centers of their respective lines. The Tenth Pennsylvania was placed in support of Easton's Battery and rendered effective aid in protecting the Federal left. The other four regiments were placed in advantageous positions. The famous "Bucktail" Regiment held a position around a brick house, near Easton's Battery, known as the Thornton House. The "Bucktail" sharpshooters took possession of this building, and from every door and window poured a destructive fire into the ranks of the Confederates. Lieutenant Colonel Kane of this regiment was severely wounded.

The ground on either side of the position of the Confederate battery was covered with woods and dense undergrowth.

STUART'S WORK

Stuart placed two of his regiments on either side of the Centreville Road, facing north. The Sixth South Carolina and the First Kentucky were to the left and the Tenth Alabama and the Eleventh Virginia to the right of the road. The South Carolina and the Kentucky regiments, in moving to their assigned positions by different routes, came into collision and, through "friendly fire," poured a destructive volley into each other—a mistake that occurred with tragic frequency in the first battles of war.

When moving forward to attack the enemy, Stuart sent a few of his cavalrymen scurrying about the country to gather the wagons and hurry them toward Centreville. The teamsters needed no further incentive to action than the startling information that the enemy might swoop down upon them at any moment. Wagons swept along the roads from every direction, the loads of hay rocking and swaying over the rough frozen ground while the air grew resonant with the vehement cries of the teamsters urging their horses to their utmost speed. Residents who witnessed the event testified that the driving done that day by the drivers was a sight not to be forgotten.

While the teams were heading tumultuously for Centreville, the opposing forces on Drane Hill were becoming more hotly engaged. The Ninth Pennsylvania, as it came into position on the Federal right, was confronted by troops partly concealed by the underbrush on their front and right. To avoid the fatal mistake of firing into friends, an injudicious member of the Ninth called out, "Are you the Bucktails?" "Yes, we are the Bucktails," came the ready response from the brush. Almost instantaneously with the response came a hot volley of musketry. The troops surmised to be "Bucktails" by the Pennsylvanians were bred in Old Kentucky, being the first Confederate regiment of that state. The confusion caused by this blunder was soon allayed, and the Ninth held its ground until the end of the fight.

Stuart, seeing his battery partially, if not wholly, disabled by the Federal fire, ordered the Sixth South Carolina and the Tenth Alabama to charge forward toward the brick house held by the "Bucktails." He hoped, by a vigorous charge upon their center, to dislodge the enemy from their strong position. These two regiments responded with alacrity, but the forward movement brought them into the open field, where they became an easy target for the sharpshooters in the Thornton House, the battery on the hill and the opposing lines of infantry. This destructive fire was too much for the Southerners, so they retired to their original position near the disabled battery.

About this time, a report reached Stuart that a large force was moving on the Washington Pike to Ord's assistance. This report was correct, for Reynolds, with the First Brigade, had started for Dranesville at the sound of the first firing. Stuart, being outnumbered and hard-pressed, and knowing that his wagons were now safely beyond the reach of the enemy, determined to withdraw. This he did without any further loss, his disabled gun being carried off by hand. The enemy made no serious attempt at pursuit, and Stuart went into camp for the night at old Frying Pan Church, about six or seven miles from the field of battle.

It is true that Stuart left the field in possession of the enemy, but had he delayed his withdrawal until the arrival of Reynolds, he would have found himself confronted by at least ten thousand troops, and his situation would have been extremely hazardous. Ord and Reynolds, gathering their dead and wounded, returned to Camp Pierpont that night. On the morning of the twenty-first, Stuart, reinforced by the Ninth Georgia and the Eighth Virginia, returned to Dranesville, but finding the Federals gone, he gathered his wounded and dead that remained and returned to Centreville.

The same uncertainty that attaches to the statistics of other battles of the war confronts us when we attempt to sum up the numbers engaged and the killed and wounded at Dranesville. Ord reported his losses as 7 killed, 61 wounded and none missing for a total of 68. Stuart reported 43 killed,

A lithograph of Federal artillery at the Battle of Dranesville.

143 wounded and 8 missing for a total of 194. The Federal forces must have numbered at least 5,000 and the Confederates between 2,000 and 2,500. The engagement lasted about two hours. The colors of the Federal regiments here engaged were taken to Washington City, and on each flag, "Dranesville, December 20, 1861" was painted in golden letters.

10

Summing Up 1861

As his state of Louisiana was preparing to leave the Union, Senator Judah Benjamin gave the following farewell speech to the Senate on New Years Eve 1860:

> *We desire, we beseech you, to let this parting be in peace...Indulge in no vain delusion that duty or conscience, interest or honor, imposes upon you the necessity of invading our States or shedding the blood of our people. You have not the possible justification for it.*
>
> *What may be the fate of this horrible contest, no man can tell...but this much, I will say: the fortunes of war may be adverse to our arms, you may carry desolation into our peaceful land, and with torch and fire you may set our cities in flame...you may, under the protection of your advancing armies, give shelter to the furious fanatics who desire, and profess to desire, nothing more than to add all the horrors of a servile insurrection to the calamities of civil war; you may do all this—and more too, if more there be—but you can never subjugate us; you never can convert the free sons of the soil into vassals, bring tribute to your power, and you never, never, can degrade them to the level of an inferior and servile race. Never! Never!*

After blood was shed at Fort Sumter and on the streets of Baltimore, after battles at Manassas, Ball's Bluff and other locations in Northern Virginia, as 1861 came to a close, this is how the nation felt, as can be seen in an editorial in the *New York Times* on January 1, 1862:

Summing Up 1861

The darkest and gloomiest year in our country's history has passed away. It opened with a portentous cloud in the Southern sky, then not bigger than a man's hand; but which has since overspread and wrapped as in a pall the whole nation.

Last New Year's Day [January 1, 1861], *only South Carolina had committed herself to dis-union; and almost everyone then thought and hoped that the process of disintegration would not go any further; but that the conservative element in the South, and the conciliatory element in the North, would speedily devise some way by which the old fraternal Union would be peacefully maintained. But before the first month had passed away, seven states were in the hands of the mutineers, and it seemed for a time almost as though the whole National fabric would tumble to pieces.*

The second month of the year shaped and compacted the revolt, by giving it a Confederated legislature and an army, and by placing at its head the adroitest of the conspirators. In April the war opened in Charleston harbor. Then followed the formation of the two great armies—by this time thirteen rebel States contributing their troops to the one, while twenty-three Union States furnished the soldiers for the other. Since then, for nine dreary months past, the progress of the national arms has been fitful and uncertain— reverse and victory checquering the record of each week.

The opening of the year found South Carolina assailant and defiant, with their clutch upon the nation's throat; its close finds her assailed, confused and desperate, with the sword of the nation planted well in her vitals. The opening of the year found a cowardly old fool and a Cabinet of knaves ruling in Washington, while the nation was doubtful even of its capital; now we have upright and courageous rulers, and half a million Republican bayonets to do their bidding. January found the nation struggling in the dark and not knowing what to do: December leaves it with a clear purpose and a fixed aim.

We begin the new year with hope, and with a consciousness of national strength which contrasts wonderfully with the dubious feeling of a year ago. And we believe that many of the weeks of the year will not pass away before light and victory will break forth over the whole country, and that, before its close, the full fruition of the nation's hopes will be realized. In this consciousness, we wish to our brave soldiers in their tents, to our gallant sailors in their ships, and to all true men the world over.

A Happy New Year.

Bibliography

PUBLICATIONS

Abramson, Rudy. *Hallowed Ground: Preserving America's Heritage.* Hong Kong: Lickle Pub. Inc., 1996.

Alexander, Bevin. *How the South Could Have Won the Civil War.* New York: Crown Publishing Group, 2007.

Alexandria Chronicle 5, no. 1 (Spring 1997); and (Fall 2008).

Cooling, Benjamin Franklin, III, and Walton H. Owen II. *Mr. Lincoln's Forts: A Guide to the Civil War Defenses of Washington.* Shippensburg, PA: Scarecrow Press, 1988.

Coski, John M. *The Confederate Battle Flag.* Cambridge, MA: Belknap Press of Harvard University Press, 2005.

Davis, Kenneth C. *Don't Know Much about the Civil War.* New York: Perennial, 1996.

Davis, William C., and the editors of Time-Life Books. *The Civil War: First Blood—Fort Sumter to Bull Run.* Alexandria, VA: Time-Life Books, 1992.

Elder, Dolores. *Uncivil Occoquan: July 27, 1860.* Occoquan, VA: The Occoquan Historical Society, 2010.

Freeman, Douglas Southall. *R.E. Lee: A Biography.* Pulitzer Prize edition. New York: Charles Scribner's Sons, 1934.

Frobel, Anne S. *The Civil War Diary of Anne S. Frobel.* McLean, VA: EPM Publications, Inc., 1986. Reprint, 1992.

Gernand, Bradley E. *A Virginia Village Goes to War: Falls Church During the Civil War.* Virginia Beach, VA: Donning Company Publishers, 2002.

Hakenson, Donald C. *This Forgotten Land (I).* Alexandria, VA: self-published, 2002.

———. *This Forgotten Land (II).* Alexandria, VA: self-published, 2011.

Henderson, G.F.R., Colonel. *Stonewall Jackson and the American Civil War.* 2 vols. New York: Da Capo Press, 1998.

Henig, Gerald S., and Eric Niderost. *A Nation Transformed: How the Civil War Changed America Forever.* Nashville, TN: Cumberland House, 2001. Reprint, 2007.

Herbert, Paul N. *God Knows All Your Names.* Bloomington, IN: Author House, 2009.

Hunter Mill Road Civil War Self-Guided Tour. Companion to the documentary film *Danger Between the Lines.* Vienna: Hunter Mill Defense League, 2008.

Hunton, Eppa. *The Autobiography of Eppa Hunton.* Richmond, VA: William Byrd Press, 1933.

The Journal of Chalkley Gillingham: Friend in the Midst of Civil War. Alexandria, VA: Alexandria Monthly Meeting, 2000.

Kundahl, George G. *Alexandria Goes to War: Beyond Robert E. Lee.* Knoxville: University of Tennessee Press, 2004.

Lee, Captain Robert E. *Recollections and Letters of Robert E. Lee by His Son, Captain Robert E. Lee.* Old Saybrook, CT: Konecky & Konecky, 1980.

Long, A.L. *Memoirs of Robert E. Lee: His Military and Personal History.* Edison, VA: General Books LLC, 1983.

McGuire, Judith W. *Diary of a Southern Refugee During the War.* Lincoln: University of Nebraska Press, 1995.

Miller, Francis Trevelyan (editor-in-chief). *The Photographic History of the Civil War in Ten Volumes.* New York: Review of Reviews Co., 1911.

Miller, William J., and Brian C. Pohanka. *An Illustrated History of the Civil War: Images of an American Tragedy.* Alexandria, VA: Time-Life Books, 2000.

Moe, Richard. *The Last Full Measure: The Life and Death of the First Minnesota Volunteers.* St. Paul: Minnesota Historical Society Press, 2001.

Muir, Dorothy Troth. *Mount Vernon: The Civil War Years.* Mount Vernon, VA: Mount Vernon Ladies' Association, 1993.

Netherton, Nan, et al. *Fairfax County, Virginia: A History.* Fairfax, VA: Fairfax County Board of Supervisors, 1978.

Poland, Charles P., Jr. *The Glories of War: Small Battles and Early Heroes of 1861.* Bloomington, IN: Author House, 2006.

Seager, Roger, II. *And Tyler Too: A Biography of John and Julia Tyler.* Charles City County, VA: Historic Sherwood Forest Corporation, 2003.

Silber, Nina. *Landmarks of the Civil War.* New York: Oxford University Press, 2003.

Trexler, Edward C., Jr. *Civil War, Fairfax Court House.* Fairfax, VA: James River Valley Publishing, 2006.

Warfield, Edgar. *Manassas to Appomattox: The Civil War Memoirs of Pvt. Edgar Warfield—17ᵗʰ Virginia Infantry.* Charlottesville, VA: Howell Press Inc., 1996.

Williams, Julia M. *Burke & Herbert Celebrates 150 Years.* Richmond, VA: The Dietz Press, 2002.

WEBSITES

Friends of Freedmen's Cemetery, www.freedmenscemetery.org.

History of Pohick Church, www.pohick.org.

History of the 17ᵗʰ Virginia Infantry, CSA, www.fairfaxrifles.org/history.html.

Lincoln at the Crossroads Alliance, www.latcra.org.

Index

About the Author

William S. Connery grew up in Baltimore, Maryland, considered to be "neutral territory" in the Civil War/War Between the States. As a young boy, his family visited the battlefields of Gettysburg, Antietam and Harpers Ferry and other local historical sites. He has a degree in history from the University of Maryland, College Park. Since 1989, Mr. Connery has lived in Fairfax County, near Old Town Alexandria, Virginia. He has contributed to the *Civil War Courier*, the *Washington Times* Civil War page and other publications. Mr. Connery is a member of the Company of Military Historians, the Capitol Hill Civil War Round Table, the Sloop of War Constellation Museum and the E.A. Poe Society of Baltimore. As a frequently requested speaker on Civil War and American history topics of that period, he speaks often in the Washington, D.C., metro region. He is married and has two sons.